Praśnāvalī

Jaḍa-Bharata's

PRAŚNĀVALĪ

A text on Advaita-Vedānta

Original text critically edited
and translated into English
by

Pranati Ghosal

With a foreword by
B. Bhattacharya

D.K. Printworld (P) Ltd.
New Delhi

Cataloging in Publication Data — DK
(Courtesy: D.K. Agencies (P) Ltd. <information@dkagencies.com>)

Jaḍabharata.
[Praśnāvalī. English & Sanskrit]
Jaḍa-Bharata's Praśnāvalī.
Includes bibliographical references (p.)
Includes index.

1. Advaita. 2. Vedanta. 3. Philosophy, Hindu.
I. Ghosal, Pranati, 1956- II. Title.

181.482 21

ISBN 81-246-0263-8 (PB)

First Published in India in 2004

Published and printed by:
D.K. Printworld (P) Ltd.
Regd. office : *'Sri Kunj'*, F-52, Bali Nagar
New Delhi - 110 015
Phones : (011) 2545-3975; 2546-6019; *Fax* : (011) 2546-5926
E-mail: dkprintworld@vsnl.net
Web: www.dkprintworld.com

Dedicated to the Holy Memory of My Preceptor

Blessings

Dr. Pranati Ghosal has critically edited and translated a Vedānta Treatise Praśnāvalī. This text, as obvious by its title, poses certain illusory questions about Reality, Absolute or individuality. These questions echo the dialogue between Rahūgaṇa and Jaḍa Bharata. These two aspects are contradictory or mutually complimentary. This text, though a small one, is important because it highlights certain so far not so much seriously taken features. It has a detailed introduction and also deals with the evaluation of the text.

This treatise is ascribed to Jaḍa Bharata who is definitely not the one who was son of Bharata but nonetheless the 18th century writer. It imbibes the spirit of the Paramahaṁsa way of carefree living. It comprises mainly fifty-two questions and these questions subsume all that could be asked in an Upaniṣadic way. The text has been translated with copious annotations and I hope the connotation of this text is accreditation to the mass of critical literaure of Vedānta.

Prof. Vidya Nivas Mishra
Member of Parliament
(Rajya Sabha)

Foreword

A SMALL tract, styled Praśnāvalī, ascribed to Bharata or Jaḍa-Bharata figures in the catalogues of Sanskrit manuscripts. Aufrecht also notes it and informs that one copy of the work lies in the Bodelian Library at Oxford. In India the manuscript is found in the libraries of the Asiatic Society, Kolkata and the Bhandarkar Oriental Research Institute, Pune.

Dr. Pranati Ghosal of the IGNCA, Varanasi centre, had selected this tract for editing, while working for M. Phil. course at the Rabindra Bharati University, Kolkata. She edited the work with the help of all the available mss., after collating the readings of all of them. The carefully edited text was lying with her all these years. The publication of the same in book-form is a commendable decision for which Dr. Ghosal deserves congratulation.

The author of the tract is shrouded in mystery. Jaḍa-Bharata or Yadu Bharata or simply Bharata is rather un-traceable. Dr. Ghosal has examined the authorship and the date of the composition of the work from all angles and has come to the conclusion that the work must belong to eighteenth century AD. Her conclusion, on the basis of information available till date, appears sound and logical.

So far as the contents of the tract is concerned, Bharata, the author appears to be a Vedāntist preacher. His only aim is to provide answers to some fundamental questions regarding the standpoint of the Vedānta, which may serve as a ready reference book. It may be conjectured that at the time of Bharata, there had been groups of *vedāntī*s attached to different *maṭhas*, for whose use these questions were conceived and answered in order to help propagate the typical views of the Vedānta School.

The linguistic and grammatical irregularities of the treatise are the natural reflection of age when Sanskrit was losing its lustre. Dr. Ghosal has carefully edited the work, pointing out the drawbacks at all places, of course maintaining the original character of the work.

I congratulate her on her academic sincerity and hope that the work will be appreciated by scholars in general and those, in particular, who want to study the course of development of the Vedānta School over the centuries. Dr. Ghosal, however, might have done well, had she provided a fully corrected text.

09.05.2003

B. Bhattacharya
Retd. Professor &
Head of Sanskrit Department,
Banaras Hindu University
Varanasi

Preface

THE present work is the critical edition of a dissertation on Praśnāvalī of Jaḍa-Bharata submitted to Rebindra Bharati University, Kolkata for M. Phil. examination. This important but less known short treatise of Monistic Vedānta still remains confined in the bundles of mss., lying in different mss. libraries of India and abroad.

During my course of study I was able to lay hand only on five copies of this work — two from Asiatic Society, Kolkata and three from Bhandarkar Oriental Research Institute, Pune. Theodor Aufrecht informs about two more copies one in the possession of Punjab University, Lahore and other in Bodelian Library, Oxford. It has not been possible for me to consult either of the two. I regret my inability.

The study reveals that there are some common errors of textual and grammatical nature and the same has been highlighted and discussed. Yet at the time of preparing text instead of giving a better and correct reading effort has been made to follow editing principles laid down in *The Introduction to the Indian Textual Criticism* by Prof. S.M. Katre. To what extent it has been successful is left to the scholars.

Ceremonial thanks giving is not befitting in the Indian tradition. But I must express my sense of gratitude to the scholars whose works I have utilized to my benefit. I am indebted to the Head of the Department of Sanskrit, Rabindra Bharati who has been pleased to allow me to carry out this work. I shall remain ever grateful to my esteemed guide Sri S.C. Goswami whose guidance and valuable instructions helped me to reach the goal. My gratitude knows no bound to all my teachers who taught me carefully and affectionately throughout the entire course. Regards to Prof. Biswanath Bhattacharya who has kindly written a foreword of this book before publication. I am indebted to the administration, the manuscript section and library of Asiatic Society Kolkata, as well as BORI who helped me generously by supplying Xerox copies of mss., and books. My sincere regards are credited to Prof. R.C. Sharma Hony. Co-ordinator IGNCA, without whose initiation this dissertation would never come to the light of day. And last of all I cannot feel content without referring to the names of my loving parents Dr. Sri Sachindra Nath Ghosal and Smt. Kanchan Mala Ghosal and my another esteemed teacher Dr. Sri S.C. Chakrabarti, Professor and Director, School of Vedic Studies under Rabindra Bharati University for their constant encouragements, inspiration and well wishes in every phase of my work.

Pranati Ghosal

Contents

Abbreviations

उप०सा०	:	उपदेश साहस्री
ऋ०	:	ऋग्वेदसंहिता
कठ०	:	कठोपनिषत्
गीता०	:	श्रीमद्भगवद्गीता
छा०	:	छान्दोग्योपनिषत्
जाबाल०	:	जाबालोपनिषत्
तै०	:	तैत्तिरीयोपनिषत्
नृसिंह०	:	नृसिंहोत्तरतापनीयोपनिषत्
पंच०	:	पंचदशी
पु० सू०	:	पुरुषसूक्त
बृहदा०	:	बृहदारण्यकोपनिषत्
मा०	:	माण्डूक्योपनिषत्
श्वेताश्व०	:	श्वेताश्वतरोपनिषत्
सर्वोप० सा० शा०	:	सर्वोपनिषत्-सारशास्त्र
A.S.	:	*Atri-Saṁhitā.*
Ā. ṭī. on Bṛh. Bhā	:	*Ānandagiri ṭīkā on Bṛhadāraṇyaka-bhāṣya*
Ātma.	:	*Ātmabodha*
Īśa.	:	*Īśopaniṣat*
Upa. Sā.	:	*Upadeśa Sāhasrī*
ṚV	:	*Ṛgveda-Saṁhitā*
Kaṭha.	:	*Kaṭhopaniṣat*
Kalpa. tī. on Bhā.	:	*Kalpataru ṭīkā on Bhāmatī*
Kṛśṇā. tī. on Si. le. sa.	:	*Kṛṣṇālaṅkāra ṭikā on Siddhāntaleśasaṁgraha*

Gītā	:	*Śrīmad Bhagavadgītā*
Chān.	:	*Chāndogyopaniṣat*
Jābāl.	:	*Jābālopaniṣat*
Tattva	:	*Tattvānusandhānam*
Taitt.	:	*Taittirīyopaniṣat*
Nṛst.	:	*Nṛsiṁhottaratāpanīyopaniṣat*
Pañca.	:	*Pañcadaśī*
Pa. ṭī. on Kalpa.	:	*Parimala ṭīkā on Kalpataru*
P.S.	:	*Puruṣasūkta*
Praśna.	:	*Praśnāvalī*
Bṛh.	:	*Bṛhadāraṇyakopaniṣat*
B.S.	:	*Brahmasūtra*
Mbh. Anu.	:	*Mahābhārata Anuśāsana-parvan*
Mbh. Ār.	:	*Mahābhārata Āraṇya-parvan*
Mbh. Śā.	:	*Mahābhārata Śānti-parvan*
Māṇḍ.	:	*Māṇḍūkyopaniṣat*
Muṇḍ.	:	*Muṇḍakopaniṣat*
Rāma. ṭī. on Pañca.	:	*Śrī Rāmakṛṣṇa ṭīkā on Pañcadaśī*
Vajra.	:	*Vajrasūcī*
V.P.	:	*Vedānta Paribhāṣā*
V.S.	:	*Vedāntasāra*
V. on Saṁ. Śā.	:	*Vyākhyā on Saṁkṣepaśārīraka*
Śā. Gran.	:	*Śāṅkara Granthamālā*
Śā. bhā. on Bṛh.	:	*Śāṅkara Bhāṣya on Bṛhadāraṇyakopaniṣat*
Śā. bhā. on B.S.	:	*Śāṅkara Bhāṣya on Brahmasūtra*
Śāvara. on J.	:	*Śāvara Bhāṣya on Jaimini-Sūtra*
Śvet.	:	*Śvetāśvataropaniṣat*
Sarva.	:	*Sarvopaniṣatsāraśāstra*
Sāra. ṭī. on Saṁ. Śā	:	*Sārasaṁgraha ṭīkā on Saṁkṣepaśārīraka*
Si. le. Sa.	:	*Siddhāntaleśasaṁgraha*
H.S.	:	*Hārīta-Saṁhitā*

1

Introduction

What is Vedānta?

THE word "Vedānta" literally means the end of the Vedas or the excellent portion of the Vedas. That is why, somewhere it is termed as *Śrutiśiraḥ* or the *Vedaśiraḥ*. This excellent portion of the Vedas, is its *Jñāna-Kāṇḍa* or the Upaniṣads. Again, it is one of the six orthodox schools of the Indian philosophy. The popularity of this school is evident from the fact that sometimes it passes for the whole of Indian philosophy. The philosophy of Upaniṣads collectively termed as Vedānta, marks the starting point of Indian philosophy, which accepts the Vedas as their supreme authority. So says Sadānanda Yogīndra in his *Vedānta-sāra,*[1] "Vedānta is that philosophy, which takes its lead from the Upaniṣads and the *Śārīrakaśāstra*[2] is instrumental to it." Brahmānanda Sarasvatī defined Vedānta in a slight,

1. वेदान्तो नाम उपनिषत् प्रमाणम्
   तदुपकारीणि शारीरकशास्त्रादीनि ॥ ३ ॥ *V.S.*, p. 8.

2. *Śārīrakaśāstra* includes the *prasthānatraya,* namely the Upaniṣads (*Śruti-prasthāna*) the *Bhagavadgītā* (*Smṛti-prasthāna*) and the *Brahma-sūtra* (*Nyāya-prasthāna*). The *Brahma-sūtra*s are the first textbook for Vedāntins. Ācārya Śaṅkara commented on this text and then his followers have given sub-commentaries and glosses. The *Brahma-sūtra*s along with these commentaries and glosses are designated as *Śārīrakaśāstra.* The word *ādi* indicates the *Rāmāyaṇa,* the *Mahābhārata,* the Purāṇas, etc. Thus the *Śārīrkaśāstra* constitutes of the *Brahma-sūtras* based on the Upaniṣads, their commentaries and other *śruti* and *smṛti* texts.

different language. His *Nyāyaratnāvalī*[3] says,

> Vedānta literature comprises of five books namely, *Śārīrakamīmāṁsā* of Vyāsa having four chapters, its commentary and gloss, the book composed by Vācaspati Miśra, i.e., Bhāmatī, its gloss *Kalpataru* and the *Parimala* — another gloss thereon.

Different Schools of Vedānta

From this disscussion, it can be safely said that *Brahma-sūtra* is the first textbook of Vedānta school, composed by Maharṣi Dvaipāyana. Śaṅkara was the first commentator on this *Brahma-sūtra*, on which we find later on two famous glosses, viz., (1) The *Pañcapādikā* and the *Vivaraṇa* thereon, and (2) the *Bhāmatī* which formed two famous sections of Advaita-Vedānta. Besides Śaṅkara, some other well-reputed scholars like Rāmānuja, Bhaṭṭa-Bhāskara, Nimbārka, etc., commented on this book and expressed different views. Now, it is difficult to ascertain which one is correct among these views. However, the difference in their views gave rise to the emergence of various schools of Vedānta in later days. They are as follows:

Brahma-sūtra

	Name of the Exponent	*Name of the School*	*Date*
1.	Śaṅkarācārya	Absolute Monism	AD 788-820
2.	Bhaṭṭa-Bhāskara	Dualistic Non-dualism of Bhāskarācārya	AD 1000
3.	Rāmānuja	Qualified Monism	AD 1140
4.	Madhvācārya	Pure Dualism	AD 1238
5.	Nimbārka	Dualistic Non-dualism of Nimbārka	Later half of 13th century
6.	Śrīkaṇṭhācārya	Qualified Monism of Śaiva-school	13th century
7.	Ballabhācārya	Pure Non-dualism	AD 1481-1533
8.	Śrījīva Goswāmī and Baladeva Vidyābhūṣaṇa	Inconceivable Dualistic Non-dualism	AD 1725

3. वेदान्तो-शास्त्रेति। शारीरकमीमांसारूपचतुरध्यायी-तद्भाष्य-तदीयटीका-वाचस्पत्य-तदीयटीका-कल्पतरुः-तदीयटीका परिमलरूपग्रन्थपंचकेत्यर्थः।

— *Nyāyaratnāvalī on Siddhāntabindu*, Benares edn., p 6.

A Brief History of Advaita Literature

Now our business is with Advaita-vedāntins, i.e., the school which followed the monistic theory of Bhagavatpāda Śaṅkarācārya. But in India the cultivation of Vedānta philosophy is not of such a recent age. It was in regular practice from pre-Bādarāyaṇa age. But it is certain that Bādarāyaṇa was the first and foremost teacher who formulated the fundamental doctrines of Vedānta in the form of *sūtra*s. In these *sūtra*s Bādarāyaṇa has mentioned occasionally the views and also the names of his predecessors like Jaimini, Āśmarathya, Bādari, Auḍulomi, Bādarāyaṇa, Kāśakṛtsna, Kārṣṇājini and Ātreya, etc., for examples,

जैमिनि	—	साक्षादप्यविरोधः जैमिनिः[4] (ब्र० सू० १/२/२८)
आश्मरथ्य	—	(1) अभिव्यक्तेरित्याश्मरथ्यः (ब्र० सू० १/२/२९)
		(2) प्रतिज्ञासिद्धेर्लिङ्गमाश्मरथ्यः (ब्र० सू० १/४/२०)
बादरि	—	(1) अनुस्मृतेर्बादरिः[5] (ब्र० सू० १/२/३०)
		(2) सुकृतदुष्कृते एवेति तु बादरिः (ब्र० सू० ३/१/११)
औडुलोमि	—	उत्क्रमिष्यत एवम्भावादित्योडुलोमिः (ब्र० सू० १/४/२१)
बादरायण	—	तदुपर्यपि बादरायणः सम्भवात् (ब्र० सू० १/३/२६)
काशकृत्स्न	—	अवस्थितेरिति काशकृत्स्नः (ब्र० सू० १/४/२२)
कार्ष्णाजिनि	—	चरणादिति चेन्नोपलक्षणार्थेति कार्ष्णाजिनिः (ब्र० सू० ३/१/९)
आत्रेय	—	स्वामिनः फलश्रुतेरित्यात्रेयः (ब्र० सू० ३/४/४४)

From this, it is clear that at least these eight teachers belonged to pre-Bādarāyaṇa age. Among them Jaimini and Bādarāyaṇa belonged to the same age and each[6] of them has

---

4. Apart from this Jaimini's view is referred to in many other *sūtra*s, e.g., 1/2/31, 1/3/31, 1/4/18, 3/2/40, 3/3/33, 3/4/2, 3/4/18, 3/4/40, 4/1/17, 4/3/12, 4/4/5, 4/4/41, etc.

5. The name of Bādari is referred to in *sūtra* nos. 1/2/30, 3/1/11, 4/3/7 and 4/4/40, etc.

6. Jaimini has quoted the view of Bādarāyaṇa in his own work: (*Pūrva-Mīmāṁsā-Sūtra*, 1.1.5).

→

quoted the view of other in his own composition. However, it is very difficult to identify the ancient teachers because there is least evidence in our hand at present to detect the exact age of our old teacher-commentators. Majority of them were religious mendicants and it is a difficult task to know the personal life of these monks. In short, the date of these *ācārya*s is yet to be questioned.

Apart from these fore-cited authors, Śaṅkara in his commentary was very frequent to refer the name of Upavarṣa,[7] the Vṛttikāra of *Brahma-sūtra*. Not only Śaṅkara, Śāvaramuni[8] also referred to his name. Later commentators like Padmapāda, Ānandagiri and even the Naiyāyika Jayantabhaṭṭa in his *Nyāya-Mañjarī* cited certain views they attribute to Upavarṣa.[9] From this it is clear, there must have been an Upavarṣa and Śaṅkara referred to his name as a member of the tradition, he follows.

Besides this, we find the name of another *Brahma-sūtra-Vṛttikāra*, he is Bodhāyana. The book *Prapañcahṛdaya*, written by an unknown author, refers to his *vṛtti* entitled *Kṛtakoṭi*. The famous Viśiṣṭādvaitin Rāmānuja occasionally cited from this *vṛtti*.

Śaṅkara mentions the name of Brahmanandin who wrote *Chāndogya* sentences (*vākyakāra*). Madhusūdana Sarasvatī, referred to his name, in his gloss on *Saṁkṣepa-śārīraka*.[10] The history of Vedānta supplies the name of another *vākyakāra*, he is Ṭaṅka. According to some critics, Ṭaṅka and Brahmanandin was the same person.

→ औत्पत्तिकस्तु शब्दस्यार्थेन सम्बन्धस्तस्य ज्ञानमुपदेशोऽव्यतिरेकश्चार्थेऽनुपलब्धे तत्प्रमाणं बादरायणस्यानपेक्षत्वात्। (१/१/५)।

Bādarāyaṇa also did the same in the fore-cited *sūtra*.

7. "वर्णा एव तु शब्द" इति भगवानुपवर्षः — *Śā. bhā. on B.S.*, 1/3/28.
8. गकारौकार विसर्जनीया इति भगवानुवर्षः — *Śāvara. on J.*, 1/1/1/5.
9. See, *Encyclopeadia of Indian Philosophy*, H. Karl Potter, vol. III, chap. 1, p. 11.
10. छान्दोग्यवाक्यकारेण ब्रह्मनन्दिनापि. . . — *Sāra. ṭī. on Saṁ. śā.*, 3/217, p. 276

From the history of Vedānta, we find the names of (1) Sundarapāṇḍyācārya the writer of *Brahmasūtra-Vṛttivārtika*, (2) Draviḍācārya, the composer of *Chāndogyopaniṣadvākya-bhāṣya*, (3) Bhartṛprapañca, who wrote *bhāṣyas* on *Kaṭha* and *Bṛhadāraṇyakopaniṣad*. Pratyaksvarūpācārya, in his *Nayana-prasādinī* gloss on *citsukhī*, referred to the name of Bhartṛhari and ascribed the book *Dhātusamīkṣā* to his name. Besides this the names of Brahmadatta and Brahmamitra, etc., are quoted in different textbooks, but the exact names of their work and their time is yet to be traced out.

In order to compose the history of literature of the Advaita School, at first we find the name of Gauḍapādācārya, the preceptor of Govindapāda, a direct teacher to Śaṅkarācārya.

GAUḌAPĀDĀCĀRYA : DATE?

Māṇḍūkyakārikā otherwise called *Gauḍapādīyakārikā*.

ŚAṄKARĀCĀRYA

AD 788-820 is roughly considered to be the age of Śaṅkarācārya. He was a resident of Kerala. His works are as follows:

1. *Śārīraka-bhāṣya,*
2. *Īśāvāsyopaniṣad-bhāṣya,*
3. *Kenopaniṣad-bhāṣya,*
4. *Kaṭhopaniṣad-bhāṣya,*
5. *Praśnopaniṣad-bhāṣya,*
6. *Muṇḍakopaniṣad-bhāṣya,*
7. *Māṇḍūkyopaniṣad-bhāṣya,*
8. *Māṇḍūkya-kārikā-bhāṣya,*
9. *Taittirīyopaniṣad-bhāṣya,*
10. *Taittirīyavārttika-bhāṣya,*
11. *Aitareyopaniṣad-bhāṣya,*

12. *Bṛhadāraṇyakopaniṣad-bhāṣya,*
13. *Bṛhadāraṇyakavārttika-bhāṣya*
14. *Chāndogyopaniṣad-bhāṣya,*
15. *Nṛsiṁhapūrvatāpanīya-bhāṣya,*
16. *Nṛsiṁhottaratāpanīya-bhāṣya,*
17. *Kauṣītakyopaniṣad-bhāṣya,*
18. *Śvetāśvataropaniṣad-bhāṣya,*
19. *Sanatsujātīya-bhāṣya,*
20. *Gītābhāṣya,* and
21. *Hastāmalaka-bhāṣya.*

Among the *prakaraṇa granthas* we find the followings:

1. *Vivekacūḍāmaṇi,*
2. *Upadeśasāhasrī,*
3. *Ātmabodha,*
4. *Tattvabodha,*
5. *Aparokṣānubhūti,*
6. *Ātmajñānopadeśavidhi,*
7. *Ajñānabodhinī*
8. *Ātmānātmaviveka,*
9. *Daśaślokī,*
10. *Śataślokī,*
11. *Māyāpañcaka,*
12. *Manīṣāpañcaka,*
13. *Advaitapañcaratna,*
14. *Pañcīkaraṇa,*
15. *Dṛgdṛśyaviveka,*

16. *Vākyavṛtti,*
17. *Laghuvākyavṛtti,*
18. *Prapañcasāra,*
19. *Vākyasudhā,* and
20. *Sarvavedāntasiddhāntasāra-saṁgraha.*

SUREŚVARĀCĀRYA

In the early stage of his life Sureśvara was supposed to be known as Maṇḍana Miśra, the reputed Mīmāṁsaka, but there is a great contradiction among the scholars whether Maṇḍana and Sureśvara was the same person.

Maṇḍana, being instructed by Kumārilabhaṭṭa met Śaṅkarācārya, in a debate. As a result of his defeat he had to become the disciple of Śaṅkara according to the previous condition of this logical encounter. This suggests that he belonged to the same age as Śaṅkara. He wrote two *vārttika*s on *Taittirīyopaniṣad* and *Bṛhadāraṇyakopaniṣad,* three textbooks namely, *Naiṣkarmyasiddhi, Brahmasiddhi* and *Svārājyasiddhi* and an essay entitled *Vidhiviveka.*

Ninth Century

SARVAJÑĀTMAMUNI

Sarvajñātman belonged to ninth century who was otherwise known as Nityabodhācārya. From AD 758-848 he was the incharge of Śṛṅgerī *maṭha.* He wrote a famous textbook on Advaita philosophy, i.e., *Saṁkṣepaśārīraka,* which he himself named as *Prakaraṇabhāṣya-vārttika.*

PADMAPĀDĀCĀRYA

He was a devoted disciple of Śaṅkarācārya and so many stories about his devotion to the master, are ascribed to his name. He wrote a famous gloss on *Śāṅkara-bhāṣya* on *Śārīrakamīmāṁsā,* namely *Pañcapādikā.*

VĀCASPATIMIŚRA

1. *Bhāmatī ṭīkā* on *Śārīraka-bhāṣya,*
2. *Brahmatattvasamīkṣā* on *Brahmasiddhi,* and
3. *Nyāyakaṇikā* on *Vidhiviveka.*

Eleventh-twelfth Century

PRAKĀŚĀTMAN

Pañcapādikāvivaraṇa, a gloss on *Pañcapādikā.*

Twelfth Century

ADVAITABODHENDRA

Brahmavidyābharaṇa.

ŚRĪ HARṢAMIŚRA

Khaṇḍanakhaṇḍakhādyam.

ĀNANDABODHABHAṬṬĀRAKA

Nyāyamakaranda, Pramāṇamālā, and *Nyāyadīpāvalī.*

Thirteenth Century

AMALĀNANDA

1. *Vedāntakalpataru,* a gloss on *Bhāmatī.*
2. *Pañcapādikādarpaṇa* on *Pañcapādikā,* and
3. *Śāstradarpaṇa.*

CITSUKHĀCĀRYA

1. *Tattvapradīpikā,*
2. *Nyāyamakarandadīpikā,*
3. *Khaṇḍanakhaṇḍakhādyadīpikā,* and
4. *Śārīraka-bhāṣya-dīpikā.*

Fourteenth Century

BHĀRATĪ-TĪRTHA : *Vaiyāsika Nyāyamālā*

It is to be noted here, according to some scholars Bhāratī-tīrtha and Vidyāraṇya was the same person. Others say, they are the preceptor and the disciple.[11]

VIDYĀRAṆYAMUNI

1. *Pañcadaśī,*
2. *Anubhūtiprakāśa,*
3. *Ṭīkā* on *Aparokṣānubhūti,*
4. *Jīvanmuktiviveka,*
5. *Vivaraṇaprameya-saṁgraha,*
6. *Dīpikā* on *Aitareyopaniṣad,*
7. *Taittirīyopaniṣad,*
8. *Chāndogyopaniṣad* and
9. *Bṛhadāraṇyakavārttikasāra.*

ŚAṄKARĀNANDA

1. *Brahma-sūtra-dīpikā,*
2. *Upaniṣadvṛtti.*

Fifteenth Century

ĀNANDAGIRI

Ṭīkā on

1. *Īśopaniṣad-bhāṣya,*
2. *Kenopaniṣad-bhāṣya,*

---

11. नत्वा श्रीभारतीतीर्थविद्यारण्यमुनीश्वरौ इति श्रीमत्परमहंसपरिव्राजकाचार्यश्री-भारतीतीर्थविद्यारण्यमुनिकृतपंचदश्याम् . . . — *Rāma. ṭī. on. Pañca.*, p. 1

3. *Kaṭhopaniṣad-bhāṣya,*
4. *Praśnopaniṣad-bhāṣya,*
5. *Muṇḍakopaniṣad-bhāṣya,*
6. *Māṇḍūkyopaniṣad-bhāṣya,*
7. *Aitareyopaniṣad-bhāṣya,*
8. *Chāndogyopaniṣad-bhāṣya*
9. *Taittirīyopaniṣad-bhāṣya,*
10. Gloss on *Taittirīyavārttika,*
11. *Bṛhadāraṇyakopaniṣad-bhāṣya,*
12. Gloss on *Bṛhadāraṇyakavārttika,*
13. *Śārīraka-bhāṣya* and
14. *Vedāntaślokī.*

PRAKĀŚĀNANDA

Siddhāntamuktāvalī

AKHAṆḌĀNANDAMUNI

Tattvadīpana on *Nyāya-makaranda.*

The Beginning of Sixteenth Century

ĀCĀRYAMALLANĀRĀDHYA

Advaitaratna, Abhedaratna.

ĀCĀRYANṚSIṀHĀŚRAMA

Advaitadīpikā, Bhāvaprakāśikā ṭīkā on *Bhedādhikāra.*

ĀCĀRYA NĀRĀYAṆĀŚRAMA

Advaitadīpikā-Vivaraṇa.

ŚRĪMAD RAṄGARĀJĀDHVARIN

He is the father and the preceptor of famous Advaita author Appayadīkṣita.[12]

Sixteenth Century

APPAYADĪKṢITA

1. *Parimala* — a gloss on *Vedānta-Kalpataru*,
2. *Siddhāntaleśasaṁgraha*, and
3. *Nyārakṣāmaṇi*.

BHAṬṬOJIDĪKṢITA

Tattvakaustubha — a gloss on *Śārīraka-bhāṣya*.

ĀCĀRYA SADĀŚIVA BRAHMENDRA

1. *Advaitavidyāvilāsa*,
2. *Bodhātmanirveda*.

It is to be noted here both these works are unpublished.

SADĀNANDAYOGĪNDRA

Vedāntasāra.

NṚSIṀHA SARASVATĪ

Subodhinī ṭīkā on *Vedāntasāra*.

VIJÑĀNA-BHIKṢU

Upadeśaratnamālā.

---

12. प्राचीनव्यवहारसिद्धविषयेष्वात्मैक्यसिद्धौ परं
संनह्यद्भिरनादरात्सरणयो नानाविधा दर्शिताः।
तन्मूलानिहसंग्रहेण कतिचित्सिद्धान्तभेदान्धियः
शुद्धयै संकलयामि तातचरणव्याख्यावचः ख्यापितान्॥ २॥
— *Si. le. Śa.*, p. 5

The Beginning of Seventeenth Century

MADHUSŪDANA SARASVATĪ

1. *Siddhāntavindu,*
2. *Saṁkṣepaśārīrakavyākhyā,*
3. *Advaitasiddhi,*
4. *Advaitaratna,*
5. *Vedāntakalpalatikā,*
6. *Gūḍhārthadīpikā ṭīkā* on *Śrīmad Bhagavad-Gītā,* and
7. *Prasthānabheda.*

RĀMATĪRTHA

Vidvan Manorañjinī ṭīkā on *Vedāntasāra.*

ĀPODEVA

Bālabodhinī ṭīkā on *Vedāntasāra.*

GOVINDADEVA

Bhāṣyaratnaprabhā ṭīkā on *Śārīraka-bhāṣya.*

RĀMĀNANDA SARASVATĪ

Vivaraṇopanyāsa.

Seventeenth Century

SADĀNANDAYATI

Advaita Brahmasiddhi.

ĀCĀRYA RAṄGANĀTHA

Vṛtti on *Śārīraka-bhāṣya.*

BRAHMĀNANDA SARASVATĪ

Laghucandrikā ṭīkā on *Advaitasiddhi.*

The Beginning of Eighteenth Century

Ācārya Acyutakṛṣṇānanda Tīrtha

1. *Kṛṣṇālaṅkāra ṭīkā* on *Siddhāntaleśa,*
2. *Banamālā ṭīkā* on *Taittirīyopaniṣad-bhāṣya*

MAHĀDEVENDRA SARASVATĪ

1. *Tattvānusandhāna,*
2. *Advaita Cintākaustubha* an autocommentary on *Tattvānusandhāna,* and
3. *Brahmasūtradīpikā.*

SADĀŚIVENDRA SARASVATĪ

1. *Ātmavidyāvalī,*
2. *Kavitākalpāvalī,* and
3. *Advaitarasamañjarī.*

Eighteenth Century

ĀYANNADĪKṢITA

Vyāsatātparyanirṇaya.

Basic Tenets of Advaita-Vedānta

Vedānta, as a philosophical system, became so popular that it passed for the whole of Indian Philosophy. Similarly sometimes by the word Vedānta, only the Advaita School is meant. But it is a common mistake to identify all the Vedānta Schools with Monistic School.

A brief discussion on the salient features of Absolute Monism will make the system prominent among others. Through the efforts of a number of diligent scholars now it can be safely said, that Śaṅkara was only a propagator of Monism and not a founder. Through his strenuous doctrine he has reestablished Monism and thereby Hinduism also. What he propagated is *Brahman*, the One, without a second is the only reality everything else being false (*brahma satyaṁjagan mithyā*). *Jīva* in his ultimate nature is nothing other than *Brahman* (*jīvobrahmaivanāparaḥ*). The non-duality of this reality cannot be established so long as the falsity of this world cannot be proved. In doing so Śaṅkara has forwarded the theory of *jīva-māyā-brahma* and thereby liberation.

According to Śaṅkara School by nature *jīva* and *Brahman* is all the same. In salvation *jīva* realizes his own nature, i.e., his oneness with *Brahman*. But elsewhere due to the influence of *māyā* he fails to realize it, feels himself separate from the Self, is compelled to enjoy pleasure and pain and remains enchained in the cycle of birth and death. *Vedāntaparibhāṣā*[13] says,

> The consciousness when limited by the external adjuncts like internal organ is termed as *pramātṛ caitanya*, i.e., the *jīva*. The same tune is being heard from *Saṁkṣepaśārīraka vyākhyā*,[14] the reflection of *cit* on the nescience, identified with *ahaṅkāra*, etc., is *jīva*.

Now we are going to have a look on Śaṅkara's view of the world. As *Brahman*, the one without a second is the only reality, so everything other than It is false. In order to prove this falsity, Śaṅkara has put forth his famous theory of *māyā*. Here a question may verily arise what is *māyā*? It is an indeterminate power of *Brahman* which is *sadasadbhyām anirvacanīyā* and *mithyābhūtasanātanī*. It is the power of *Brahman* in distinguishable from It, just as the burning power of the fire is, from the fire itself. It is by this power *Brahman* conjures up the whole world with all its varieties and variations. Just as the cobweb

---

13. अन्तःकरणावच्छिन्नं चैतन्यं प्रमातृचैतन्यम्।

— *V.P.*, Chap. 1, p. 16

14. अहंकारतादात्म्यापन्नाज्ञानप्रतिबिम्बत्वं जीवत्वमिति।

— *V. on Saṁ. Śā.*, 2/176, p. 318

issues forth from the juices of the spider with the effort of the spider itself, just as the medicinal herbs grow over the earth, just as the nails and hairs of man grow by nature, so also the world comes out of *Brahman* by the magical power of *māyā*. So says *Muṇḍakopaniṣad*[15] boldly.

Hence the world being a product of *māyā* has no eternal reality, but bears an empirical reality only. So long as the Transcendental Reality is not realized there is no reason to deny it. But with the dawn of Transcendental Reality the world show vanishes just as the objects of dream disappear after waking up.

The sole theory of Advaita metaphysics is *nirguṇa Brahman*. It is *saccidānandasvarūpaḥ* (Being-Consciousness-Bliss as such). But it is not existent, conscious and blissful as these are not Its qualities. It is Being as such, Consciousness as such and Bliss as such. There is no substantive-attributive relationship (*guṇaguṇi sambandhaḥ*) between them. Being[16] is that which cannot be negated. Moreover, *Brahman* is *citsvarūpaḥ*. It is self-luminous. No separate cause of Its manifestation can be concerned. Revelation is Its very nature. Again It is Bliss as such. It is beyond all determination and differences (*sajātīya-vijātīya-svagata bhedarahitaḥ*). So *nirguṇa Brahman* is the Highest Turth, the only reality, which destroys nescience and makes *jīva* liberated. The self-reliant passes over the misery of this world. This *Brahman* is Emanent as well as Transcendent. The description of *Brahman* as Real, Conscious and Infinite, is an attempt to describe Its essence. *Māyā* is attributed to It from the lower point, i.e., the creator, etc. Then It becomes the

---

15. यथोर्णनाभिः सृजते गृह्णते
 यथा पृथिव्यामोषधयः सम्भवन्ति ।
 यथा सतः पुरुषात् केशलोमानि
 तथाऽक्षरात् सम्भवतीह विश्वम् ॥
 — *Muṇḍ.*, 1/1/7, p. 18

16. सत्यत्वं वाधराहित्यम् . . . — *Pañca.*, 3/29, p. 89

saguṇa Brahman. The knowledge of *saguṇa Brahman* purifies the worshipper but by knowing the Indeterminate *Brahman* one attains liberation being identical with It.

In short, this Liberation is nothing other than the immediate awareness and realization of Self devoid of the adjunct of the knower-known and the knowledge as well as of all the relations and processes. *Mokṣa* is self-complete and self-effulgent. It is not the production of anything new, nor the purification of any old state, but the realization[17] of that, which is always there being not known, even in the stage of bondage. It is just like the finding of one's necklace on one's own neck who has forgotten its existence there and searched hither and thither. As the bondage is due to an illusion It is not merely the absence of any misery but a state of positive Bliss. Because *Brahman* is Bliss and Liberation is nothing other than *Brahman* but identical with It. To the liberated soul, the whole of Cosmos sinks in *Brahman*. He is incessantly overwhelmed with It. He sees nothing over than Himself. He sees Himself in all and all in Himself. He faces no grief, no lamentation. He is above all bondage and limitations. Such is the declaration of *Īśopaniṣad*.[18]

Nature of the Work

There are lots of works of the Monistic school of Vedānta unpublished yet, and they are preserved in the manuscript libraries of India and abroad. In recent days, it has been easy

---

17. आत्मा तु सततं प्राप्योऽप्राप्तवदविद्यया।
तन्नाशे प्राप्तवद्भाति स्वकण्ठाभरणं यथा॥ ४४॥
— *Ātma. Śā. gran.* vol. III, p. 211

18. यस्तु सर्वाणि भूतान्यात्मन्येवानुपश्यति।
सर्वभूतेषु चात्मानं ततो न विजुगुप्सते॥ ६॥
यस्तु सर्वाणि भूतान्यात्मैवाभूद्विजानतः।
तत्र को मोहः क्व शोकः एकत्वमनुपश्यतः॥ ७॥
— *Īśa*, pp. 15-16

to get ready information about them with the aid of the descriptive Catalogues of mss., *The Catalogus Catalogorum* and the works alike. While consulting *The Descriptive Catalogue of Manuscripts of the Asiatic Society*, vol. XI, 1957 the title of this work drew attention of the present editor and ultimately inspired her to proceed to the work of editing the text.

The materials for editing the present text are five manuscripts two of which have been collected from the library of The Asiatic Society, Kolkata and three others from that of Bhandarkar Oriental Research Institute, Pune. According to the information of *The New Catalogus Catalogorum*, vol. VII, p. 178, three copies of this text, are preserved in the manuscript library of the Deccan College, bearing the Cat. Nos. 511, 512 and 520. But on enquiry it was known that all these copies were deposited later on in the mss. library of BORI, Pune. According to Theodor Aufrecht there are two mss. of this text, one in the Punjab University, Lahore, and the other in the Bodelian Library, Oxford. However, the present editor had no opportunity to have the copies of the last named two mss. Therefore it was not possible for her to consult those mss. for editing the present text.

For this critical edition, the present scholar had five mss. totally, which were named as AS-1, AS-2, BORI-1, 2 and 3 respectively, according to their source where from they have been collected.

Though the present text is the outcome of the careful collation of all the five mss. owing to their completeness and general accuracy, still AS-1, AS-2 and BORI-2 are more helpful in the task of this text construction for their relatively more accurate readings. Text no. 3 and 5, i.e., BORI-1 and 3 contain a few erroneous readings. The reading of our concerned text has been altered by them (BORI-1 and 3), where they incorporate better or clear reading or the fore-cited three copies read erroneously. The suggested proper reading has been presented in the footnote, where the basic texts have been altered. The spelling mistakes also have been corrected according to the necessity. It is interesting to note here that all the mss. contain texts almost similar in length with slight variations here and there.

Application of genealogical method in the construction of text is not possible here, because there is no such clue as to determine the line of transmission of mss. Internal evidence also doesn't supply any data, on the basis of which we may determine the position of the manuscripts. Therefore all the five manuscripts are taken as equally important containing individual merit in determining the "archetype," i.e., the exact copy of the text intended by the author.

Description of the Materials

AS-1

It is a laminated paper ms. found in the Asiatic Society Library Calcutta, bearing the Cat. No. G.C. 341, 10 × 5" in size, containing 9 folio having 12 lines on each page. The appearance is old yet tolerable though worm-eaten in some places. By nature it is a complete ms. containing generally correct readings and the used script is Nāgara. It begins with:

ॐ श्री गणेशाय नमः।

सच्चिदानन्दमात्मानमद्वयाखण्डमच्युतम्।
ध्यात्वा प्रश्नावली सम्यक् क्रियते मोक्षसिद्धये॥

The colophon of the ms. reads as:

इति श्रीमत्परमहंसपरिव्राजकाचार्य श्रीमुनि माधवानन्दस्य शिष्यस्य जड़भरत विरचिता प्रश्नावली समाप्ता।

AS-2

It is a country made paper ms. lying in the same library bearing the Cat. No. G.C. 9560, 13 × 5" in size, containing 6 folio having 11 lines, on each page. It is also written in neat Nāgara script. Appearance is fresh. It contains generally correct reading and complete. It begins with:

ॐ श्री गणेशाय नमः।

सच्चिदानन्दमात्मानमद्वयाखण्डमच्युतम्।
ध्यात्वा प्रश्नावली सम्यक् क्रियते मोक्षसिद्धये॥

The colophan reads as:

इति श्रीमत्परमहंसपरिव्राजकाचार्य श्रीमुनि माधवानन्दस्य शिष्यस्य जड़-भरत विरचिता प्रश्नावली समाप्ता। राम संवत् १८९१ शुभम्।

The colophon of this ms. contains the date of the scribe but nothing about his name or any whereabouts.

BORI-1

It is a country made paper ms. found in Bhandarkar Oriental Research Institute, Pune bearing Cat. no. 284 of 1895-98 with new No. 27, 12 × 5" in size, consisting of 23 folio, having 7 lines on the each page. Generally written in Nāgara script. Contains plenty of incorrect readings. Appearance is fresh but the scribe's handwriting is illegible. It is interesting to note here, that all the mss. present 52 questions at first beginning with कान्यनुवन्धानि, का प्रकृतिः, etc., and then give their answers respectively. In this case it is to be noted that at first all the questions have been put forth, then at the time of answering each of the questions is repeated once again. It begins with usual benedictory verse:

ॐ श्री गणेशाय नमः।

सच्चिदानन्दमात्मानमद्वयाखण्डमच्युतम्।
ध्यात्वा प्रश्नावली सम्यक् क्रियते मोक्षसिद्धये॥

The colophon reads as follows:

इति श्रीमत् परमहंस परिव्राजकाचार्य मुनि माधवानन्दस्य शिष्य भरतविरचितायां प्रश्नावली समाप्तम्। नारायणं पद्मभवं वशिष्टं सक्तिंच ततपुत्र पारासुरंच व्यासं सुखं गोड़पाद महन्त गोविन्द योगीन्द्रमथ सशिष्यं इति श्रीमत् शंकराचार्यमथा सपद्मपादन्तहस्तामलकंच शिष्यं त्रोटकं वारत्यवारमनेनिसमद्गुरं सन्ततं नतोस्मी॥

The name or the date of the scribe is not found in the text.

BORI-2

It is a country made paper ms. lying in BORI, Pune with Cat. No. 287 of 1895-98 with new No. 21, 10 × 5" in size, consisting of 10 folio having 11 lines on each page. Written in neat Nāgara script. Appearance is fresh complete. It begins with:

ॐ श्री गणेशाय नमः।

सच्चिदानन्दमात्मानमद्वयाखण्डमच्युतम्।
ध्यात्वा प्रश्नावली सम्यक् क्रियते मोक्षसिद्धये॥
अथ वेदान्त लिख्यते।

It is curious to note here, that the name of the work mentioned at first differs in the same ms. at the end. The title page shows the name प्रश्नोत्तरावली टीका whereas colopnon presents the name as प्रश्नावली व्याख्या।

The colophon reads as:

इति श्रीमत् परमहंस परिव्राजकाचार्य श्रीमुनि माधवानन्दस्य शिष्येण जड़भरतविरचिता प्रश्नावली व्याख्या समाप्ता। संवत् १८०४। शुभं भूयात्।

BORI-3

It is a country made paper ms. found from BORI, Pune, containing the Cat. No. 120 of 1902-07 with new No. 23, 16 × 6" in size consisting of 10 folio having 11 lines on each page. Written in Nāgara script. It contains plenty of incorrect readings. Appearance is fresh but the hand writing is illegible. It begins with

ॐ श्री गणेशाय नमः।
सच्चिदानन्दमात्मानमद्वयाखण्डमच्युतम्।
ध्यात्वा प्रश्नावली सम्यक् क्रियते मोक्षसिद्धये॥

It is interesting to note here that the colophon of this ms. presents the name, place and the date of the scribe in details.

The colophon reads as:

इति श्रीमत् परमहंस परिव्राजकाचार्य श्रीमुनि माधवानन्दस्य शिष्येण जड़भरतविरचिता प्रश्नावली व्याख्या समाप्ताम्।संवत् १८८०।

माधमासे शुक्लपक्षे तिथौएकादस्यां बुधवासरे।
लिखतं मिश्र भवानीसंकरेदत्तेन इन्द्रप्रस्थे मध्ये॥ शुभमस्तु।

The Author : Personal Life and Date

Here, the concerned text, *Praśnāvalī* is ascribed to one Jaḍa-Bharata. Dr. Raghavan,[19] in his work, mentions the name of the author of the said text as Jaḍa-Bharata, Yadubharata and Bharata. Only one manuscript reads the name as Bharata[20] and four other mss. mention the name as Jaḍa-Bharata. But none of them supports the name Yadubharata. However, another copy of this manuscript which is lying in Bodelian Library,[21] Oxford, supports the name of the author as Yadubharata.

For want of sufficient materials it is very difficult to focus on the personal life of our teacher-commentator-writers. Because majority of such writers were religious mendicants and they left least evidence to trace out their whereabouts and Jaḍa-Bharata is no exception to this tradition. However, Jaḍa-Bharata, at the end of his work refers himself, as the pupil of one Mādhavānanda Muni.[22] But no information about this Mādhavānanda is available now. In fact, he has left nothing for us about this point. The only fact we can know is that, *Praśnāvalī* is Jaḍa-Bharata's sole work. We don't find any other work attributed to him. The manuscripts don't throw any light on his place either. As the manuscripts are scattered throughout

---

19. V. Raghavan, *New Catalogus Catalogorum*, vol. VII, p. 178.
20. Ms. No. 3, i.e., BORI-1 mentions the name of the author as Bharata.
21. A German scholar E. Hultzsch in his *Notices on Indian Manuscripts*, mentions the name of the author of *Praśnāvalī* as Yadubharata. According to this notice, the collection of mss. mentioned therein, have been purchased by Bodelian Library, Oxford. Hultzsch's notices have been published in *ZDMG*, vol. 40, part 1, p. 12.
22. The colophon of all the mss. except No. 3 show,

    इति श्रीमत् परमहंसपरिव्राजकाचार्य श्रीमुनि माधवानन्दस्य शिष्यो जड़भरत विरचिता प्रश्नावली समाप्ता।

India or abroad, it is difficult to suppose anything about it. So the history of Jaḍa-Bharata still remains, a matter of further investigation.

As regards his time, we may cite some evidence for hypothetical conclusion. Jaḍa-Bharata, in his work mentions the name of one Viśveśvara,[23] who prescribes the rules for the mendicants, attached to the path of Monistic Vedānta. His work entitled *Viśveśvarīpaddhati* or *Yatisandhyāvidhi*, still remains unpublished. But the date of Viśveśvara itself is uncertain. Therefore it does not help us in ascertaining the date of Jaḍa-Bharata. However, there are quotations from *Pañcadaśī*, in this text and this proves, that Jaḍa-Bharata flourished after Vidyāraṇya, the illustrated author of *Pañcadaśī*. Some passages of *Praśnāvalī*, divulge similarity with the text of *Tattvānusandhāna* of Mahādevendra Sarasvatī. *Tattvānusandhāna* is a merited text dealing with the topics of Advaita-Vedānta in details and it is likely that Jaḍa-Bharata was influenced by Mahādevendra Sarasvatī. In that case, Jaḍa-Bharata becomes a modern writer, belonging to a period not earlier than seventeenth century AD. Nothing more can be said about the date of Jaḍa-Bharata.

Evaluation of the Text

The entire text deals with 52 questions concerning the doctrines of Advaita-Vedānta and their relevant answers. But the treatment of the questions and their answers, as it appears is not made in a systematic way. Only the first nine questions and their answers, as pointed out in the traditional texts like *Pañcadaśī*, *Vedāntasāra*, etc., are in proper order. After that Jaḍa-Bharata is found shifting the topics from one context to another rapidly, e.g., now he asks "What is meant by the term *viparyaya*"[24] and then proceeds to discuss "What is *Brahman*?"

---

23. सम्प्रदायमार्गेण विश्वेश्वरीय वृत्त्यनुसारेण . . .
— *Praśna*, 31, p. 39

24. किं विपर्ययः ? ।२९। किं ब्रह्म ?। ३०। — *Praśna*, p. 31.

From the text, it would appear, that the questions were raised by the disciples and their solutions were put forth by the preceptor, in course of discussion. Therefore it was not possible for our author to maintain the proper order.

In some places Jaḍa-Bharata appears to answer the same[25] question simply in a different style. Moreover in order to define different technical terms of Monistic Philosophy like *ātman, svarūpa, vastu,* Jaḍa-Bharata is found to discuss the same topic represented in a slight different language. Here the author has used three different terms only, perhaps to aviod repitition. But to answer the questions he meant the same thing, i.e., the Soul.

In answering the questions Jaḍa-Bharata does not show any originality and follows the classical texts as well as renowned texts of Vedānta. For example, in order to answer the questions like "What is *prakṛti*[26] ? "What is *māyā* ?" "What is *avidyā*?" "Which are the non-quintuplicated five rudimentary elements?" "How are they created?" "What are their names?" Jaḍa-Bharata quotes from famous *śruti*-texts as well as from the traditional Vedānta texts like *Vedāntasāra,*[27] *Pañcadaśī,*

---

25. किं सोपाधिको भ्रमः ? । किं निरुपाधिको भ्रमः ? । कः भ्रमः ? । को बन्ध ? — *op. cit.,* p. 31.

26. का प्रकृतिः ? ।२। का माया ? ।३। का अविद्या ? ।४। कान्यपंचीकृत पंचभूतानि ? ।५। तेषां कथमुत्पत्तिः किं नामकानि च । ? ।६।

27. In order to answer Q. No. 2, "What is *prakṛti*" ? Jaḍa-Bharata imitates the style of *Pañca* & *VS* and quotes from *Śvet.* 1/3, (p. 19)

    "ते ध्यानयोगानुगता अपश्यन्

    देवात्मशक्तिं स्वगुणैर्निगूढम्" ।

    The answere of Q. No. 3 & 4, are prepared following the style of *Pañca,* 1/15-16. Here we find a quotation from *NṚST,* Chap. 9, p. 30.

    "माया चाविद्या च स्वयमेव भवतीति ।"

    In order to answer Q. No. 6. Our writer simply quotes from →

Sarvavedāntasiddhāntasāra-saṁgraha, Siddhāntaleśasaṁgraha, etc., in support of his statements.

In theory and technique, deviation from the tradition is noticed in very few cases. For example, in order to define "who is brāhmaṇa?[28] Does it refer to the being or the caste or the colour or the scholarship or the action or the body"? Our author boldly refutes all the possible alternatives and comes to his own conclusion.

In this connection it may be mentioned that it was a practice among the different scholars of different schools to raise points concerning the definition of brāhmaṇa, e.g., in the *Assalāyana Sutta*[29] of *Majjhima Nikāya,* claims of brāhmaṇas as the superior class, have been proved baseless and thereby brāhmaṇahood has been refuted. Similarly Aśvaghoṣa in his *Vajrasūcī*[30] refuted the brāhmaṇahood of being, caste, colour, action, scholarship and body and concludes, "Abstinence from all sins is Brāhmaṇahood which is as white as *kunda*-flower. . ."[31] It is said, "He who is free from selfishness, free from the sentiment of egoism, free from attachment, he who is without any possession, free from lust and hatred, is recognized as brāhmaṇa by the gods." The *Vajrasūcikopaniṣat*[32] also dealt the same topic in the same way.

Now a question may verily arise, had the topic been

→ *Taitt.*, 2/1/1, p. 56. "तस्माद्वा एतस्मादात्मन आकाशः सम्भूतः आकाशाद्वायुर्वायोरग्निरग्नेरापो अद्भ्यः पृथिवी" चेत्यादि श्रुतेरेवं तेषामुत्पत्तिः ।

28. *Praśna.*, 10, pp. 33f.

29. (i) *Majjhima Nikāya.*, Chap. 44, p. 203.

    (ii) *Dictionary of Pāli Proper Names.*, G.P. Malalasekara, p. 208.

30. "ब्राह्मणत्वं न शास्त्रेण न संस्कारैर्न जातिभिः ।
    न कुलेन न वेदेन न कर्मणा भवेत्ततः ॥" *Vajra*, p. 4

31. "कुन्देन्दुधवलं हि ब्राह्मणत्वं नाम सर्वपापस्यापाकरणमिति ।" — *loc. cot.*

32. *Vajrasūcikopaniṣat*, 1, *Ja.*, p. 11.

handled so frequently, what more Jaḍa-Bharata had to say on this point? Moreover, there is nothing unique in his conclusion as it is found in the Upaniṣads,[33] Śaṅkara's[34] commentary on *Bṛhadāraṇyakopaniṣat*, Ānandagiri's[35] gloss on the aforesaid commentary, Amalānanda's[36] *Kalpataru* on *Bhāmatī*, etc. Then what did Jaḍa-Bharata contribute here?

In answer it can be said that though the topic had been handled so frequently by various scholars, still his technique of handling the theory and style of presentation is unique. In each of the fore-cited works specially in *Assalāyanasutta* and *Vajrasūcī* non-Vedic scholars intended to refute the brāhmaṇahood and not to establish it. But Jaḍa-Bharata's task was to refute all the *prima facie* views, irrespective of non-Vedic orthodox schools and at the same time to define the term more logically. Though his process of refutation is based on the logic of non-Vedic scholars yet he didn't accept their views ultimately. He tried to establish the traditional theory

---

33. (i) तस्माद्ब्राह्मणः पाण्डित्यं निर्विद्य बाल्येन तिष्ठासेत्। वाल्यंच पाण्डित्यंच निर्विद्याथ मुनिरमौनंच मौनंच निर्विद्याथ ब्राह्मणः। — *Bṛh*, 3/5/1, p. 448

    (ii) "य एतदक्षरं" गार्गि विदित्वाऽस्माल्लोकात् प्रैति स ब्राह्मणः — *Ibid.*, 3/8/10, p. 489

    (iii) "नैनं पाप्मा दहति, सर्वं पाप्मानं तपति, विरजो विपापो अविचिकित्सो ब्राह्मणो भवति।" — *Ibid.*, 4/4/23, p. 499

34. ब्राह्मणो ब्रह्मवित्, पाण्डित्यं पाण्डित्यभावमेतदात्मविज्ञानं निःशेषं कृत्वेत्यर्थः . . . पाण्डित्यवाल्यसंज्ञको निःशेषं कृत्वा मौनं नामात्मप्रत्ययतिरस्करणस्य पर्यवसानं फलं तच्च निर्विद्याथ ब्राह्मणः कृतकृत्यो भवति, ब्रह्मैव सर्वमिति प्रत्ययः उपजायते।"
    — *Śā. bhā on Bṛh*, 3/5/1, p. 464

35. महावाक्यार्थावगतिर्हि ब्राह्मण्यम् —
    — *Ā. ṭī. on Bṛh. bhā*, 3/5/1, p. 465

36. मौनादन्यत् बाल्यं पाण्डित्यममौनं मौनंच निदिध्यासनं निर्विद्याथ ब्राह्मणः। ब्रह्माहमित्यवगच्छतीति ब्राह्मणः साक्षात्कृतब्रह्मा भवतीत्यर्थः।
    — *Kalpa. ṭī. on Bhā.*, 3/4/47

    ब्रह्म अणति अवगच्छतीति ब्राह्मणः।
    — *Pa. ṭī. on Kalpa.*, 3/4/47

but not in the traditional way. His conclusion is totally free from the influence of traditional Vedic scholars so far as the interpretation of the term "brāhmaṇa" is concerned.

Traditional Vedic scholars and *smṛti*-writers accepted that brāhmaṇahood can be ascertained by birth[37] or by scholarship[38] or by colour.[39] But Jaḍa-Bharata in spite of his being the writer of a later date, was not shaky under the influence of these writers and dared to uphold the Upaniṣadic theory in more logical way. Herein lies his originality.

The text divulges in some cases remarkable similarity with *Tattvānusandhāna* of Mahādevendra Sarasvatī: In order to discuss "What is to be meant by the term 'infinity' Jaḍa-Bharata is found to imitate the answer from the passage of *Tattvānusandhāna*."[40]

Further it is interesting to note that in spite of the similarity of Jaḍa-Bharata's text with that of Mahādevendra Sarasvatī, *Praśnāvalī* cannot be regarded as a duplicate copy of *Tattvānusandhāna* as its points of deviation from the aforesaid text are distinct. In course of narrating different topics he has

---

37. (i) " जन्मना ब्राह्मणः ज्ञेयः संस्काराद्विज उच्यते।
वेदपाठाद्भवेद्विप्रो श्रोत्रियस्त्रिभिरेव च॥" — *A.S.*, 140, p. 9
(ii) "ब्राह्मण्या" ब्राह्मणेनैवमुत्पन्नो ब्राह्मणो स्मृतः। — *H.S.*, 15, p. 122
(iii) "ब्राह्मण्यां" ब्राह्मणाज्जातः स्यान्न संशयः"।
— *MBh. Anu.*, 13/47/28, p. 286

38. "सर्वे सर्वास्वपत्यानि जनयन्ति सदा नराः
वाङ्मिथुनमथो जन्म मरणंच समं नृणाम्॥
तावच्छूद्रो सम ह्येष यावद्वेदे न जायते"।
— *MBh. Ār.*, 3/177/27, p. 604

39. "ब्राह्मणानां सितवर्णो क्षत्रियाणांच लोहितम्।
वैश्यानां पीतको वर्णः शूद्राणामसितस्तथा॥"
— *MBh. Śā.*, 12/181/5, p. 1024

40. *Praśna.*, 51, p. 46, cf. *Tattva*, chap. 1, p. 13.

shortened/modified, somewhere twisted the statements of Mahādevendra Sarasvatī, in order to propagate his favourite theory. For example, *Tattvānusandhāna*[41] defines the term *saṁnyāsa* in the traditional way, discussed its various divisions in details and pointed out necessary qualifications required for allowing different stages of *saṁnyāsa*. Jaḍa-Bharata in his text discussed the topic in an abridged form and presented only its four divisions and characteristic propensities required for attaining different types of *saṁnyāsa*,[42] viz., *kuṭīcara, bahūdaka, haṁsa* and *paramahaṁsa*. In this connection, it may be mentioned that Mahādevendra Sarasvatī allowed women also to be initiated into *saṁnyāsa*.[43] With regard to this particular

---

41. विहितानां कर्मणां विधिना परित्यागः संन्यासः। स च वैराग्यहेतुकः। "यदहरेव विरजेत्तदहरेव प्रव्रजेदित्यादि श्रुतेः। वैराग्यं परमेतस्य मोक्षस्य परमोऽवधिरिति श्रुतेश्च। स वैराग्यतारतम्येन चतुर्विधः। कुटीचकवहूदकहंसपरमहंसभेदात्। वैराग्यं द्विविधमपरं परंचेति। तत्रापरं चतुर्विधं यतमानव्यतिरेकैन्द्रियत्ववशीकार भेदात्। . . . वशीकारवैराग्यमैहिकामुष्मिकविषयजिहासा। तत्रिविधं मन्दं, तीव्रं, तीव्रतरंचेति। तीव्रवैराग्ये सति यात्राद्यशक्तौकुटीचकाधिकारः तच्छक्तो बहूदकसंन्यासाधिकारः, तीव्रतरवैराग्ये सति हंससंन्यासाधिकारः। एते सन्न्यासास्त्रयः। . . . तीव्रतरवैराग्येसति मुमुक्षोः परमहंससंन्यासाधिकारः, स च परमहंसी द्विविधः, विविदिषा संन्यासः विद्वत्संन्यासश्चेति। साधनसम्पन्नेन तत्त्वमुद्दिश्य क्रियमाणो संन्यासः विविदिषासंन्यासः . . . स द्विविधः जन्मापादककर्मत्यागात्मकः प्रैषोच्चारणपूर्वकदण्डधारणाद्याश्रमरूपश्चेति। विरक्तस्य गृहस्थादेः प्रयत्ननिमित्तवशेन संन्यासप्रतिबन्धे सति आद्यसंन्यासेऽधिकारः। अत्र स्त्रीणामप्याधिकारः।. . .

— *Tattva.*, chap. 2, p. 22-23

42. संन्यासश्चतुर्विधः। तीव्रवैराग्ययुक्तस्यं कुटीचरो बहूदको वा संन्यासः शास्त्रेणोच्यते। तीव्रतरवैराग्ययुक्तस्यात्मानात्मविवेदरूपो विधिपूर्वको हंससंन्यासोऽभिधीयते। शास्त्रे परं वैराग्ययुक्तस्य ब्रह्मज्ञानोत्तरकाले विधिना शिखासूत्रादित्यागरूपः परमहंससंन्यासोऽयमेव विद्वत्संन्यास इत्युच्यते। यथायोग्योऽयं संन्यासार्थः।

— *Praśna*, 44, p. 42

43. विविदिषा संन्यासः द्विविधः। जन्मापादककर्मत्यागात्मकः, प्रैषोच्चारणपूर्वकदण्ड-धारणाद्याश्रमरूपश्चेति। . . . विरक्तस्य गृहस्थादेः प्रयत्ननिमित्तवेशन संन्यासप्रतिबन्धे सति आद्यसंन्यासेऽधिकारः। अत्र स्त्रीणामप्यधिकारः।

— *Tatta.*, chap. 2, p. 23

point Jaṭa-Bharata kept silence. It may be an indication that he was not in favour of the women to attain the order of *saṁnyāsa*.

As the text says, our author takes liberty of introducing some technical terms like *upasatti*, *ekaparatva*, etc., which are less known in the classical or Vedānta texts. In the Upaniṣads[44] and other Vedānta texts like *Siddhāntaleśasaṁgraha*,[45] etc., we find the use of the term *upasadana* but not *upasatti* in the sense of going or approaching the teacher to learn any branch of knowledge. According to the derivation *upasatti* should mean same as *upasadanam* but Jaḍa-Bharata used the term in a slight different way.[46] By this term he wanted to mean, not only to approach the teacher but also to receive the instructions from the preceptor in the prescribed way. In the same way he used the term *ekaparatva*,[47] in the sense to be fully occupied with one engrossed in it. Bhāratītīrtha in *Pañcadaśī* and Mahādevendra Sarasvatī in *Tattvānusandhāna* explained the same idea but didn't use the same term. In order to define this

44. तस्मै सविद्वानुपसन्नाय प्रशान्तचित्ताय शमान्विताय . . .

— *Muṇḍ.*, 1/2/13, p. 18

45. (i) न च तद्विज्ञानार्थं स गुरूमेवाभिगच्छेदिति गुरुपसदनविधिनैव गुरूरहितविचारव्यावृत्तिसिद्धेः . . . *Si. le. Sa.*, Chap. 1, p. 19

(ii) गुरुपसदनं गुर्वभिगमनमित्यर्थः — *Kṛṣṇā.*, *ṭī. on Si. le. sa.*, ch. 1, p. 19

46. सम्प्रदायमार्गेण विश्वेश्वरीय वृत्त्यनुसारेण विधिपूर्वकं हंससंन्यासादि मानससंन्यासपर्यन्तं विधिपूर्वकं ब्रह्मनिष्ठागुरोरुपदेशः गृह्यते सा उपसत्तिः।

Praśna., 31, p. 39

47. कस्यचिद्भाग्यमतो ब्रह्मणश्चिन्तनादौ सुरुचिर्वर्धते तदेक-परत्वम्।
यथा, पतिव्रतायाः पतिचिन्तनादौ रुचिर्भवति। तदुक्तं,

"तच्चिन्तनं तत्कथनमन्योन्यं तत्प्रबोधनम्।
एतदैक्य परत्वंच ब्रह्माभ्यासं विदुर्वुधाः॥"

Praśna, 32, p. 39

point Bhāratītīrtha used the term *Brahmābhyāsa*[48] while Mahādevendra Sarasvatī termed it as *abhyāsa*[49] only, which is a means to attain *jīvanmukti.*

Moreover the text shows some peculiar sentential applications, which are grammatically incorrect.[50] It doesn't mean that the author lacks grammatical knowledge. Perhaps his intention was to express the secret doctrines of Advaitism to the pupils and in doing so he became somewhat perplexed, as the thoughts became intricate and couldn't maintain alertness about the grammatical usage.

The novelty of this text lies in its question-answer technique for both teaching and propagation of Advaita doctrines in an easy way. If someone wants to be acquainted with the theories of Monistic Vedānta in a general way not going through the voluminous works of famous authors like, Śaṅkara, etc., this work will help him immensely. Again this work will serve a meaningful purpose even to a devotee, who is not qualified enough to understand the intricate theories of

---

48. *Pañca*, 7/106, p. 278.

49. सोऽयं जीवन्मुक्तिस्तत्वभानवासनाक्षयमनोनाशाऽभ्यासात् सिध्यति। उत्पन्नस्य तत्त्वज्ञानस्य अभ्यासो नाम पुनः पुनः केनाप्युपायेन तत्त्वाऽनुसंधानम्।

— *Tattva.*, chap IV, p. 41

50. Text No. 13. Here the language of the text is cumbrous and grammatically incorrect.

"यथा स्फटिकं शुद्धमपिज्ञातं रक्तपुष्पादिसमीपकसम्बन्धाल्लोहितत्ववद्भाति तद्वत् ज्ञानिना आत्मा शुद्धमपि ज्ञातं प्रारब्धवशाद्विश्वकर्तृत्वादि अन्तःकरणसम्बन्धात् प्रपंचादिवद्भातीति सोपाधिको भ्रमः।"

Praśna, 13, p. 35

The correct reading should be as follows:

"यथा स्फटिकं शुद्धं ज्ञातमपि रक्तपुष्पादिसमीपकसम्बन्धाल्लोहितत्ववद्भाति, तद्वत् ज्ञानिना आत्मा शुद्धतया ज्ञातोऽपि प्रारब्धवशात्तस्य विश्वकर्तृत्वादि अन्तःकरणसम्बन्धात् स प्रपंचादिवद्भातीति सोपाधिको भ्रमः।"

Advaitism on his own from the works which are famous and widely circulated. Thus Jaḍa-Bharata deserves credit for creating interest in Advaitism among the people belonging to the community of both the learners and the devotees. Smallness of the work is another point of Jaḍa-Bharata's credit. Though small in size the work covers almost all the important topics expected to be known by a devotee or by a learner. Jaḍa-Bharata is conscious about the fear-psychosis which an ordinary learner of average merit faces while taking pains in going through the voluminous works of Advaita-Vedānta and his kind heart inspired him to devise a short-cut and easy method for the beginners of this branch of learning and that Jaḍa-Bharata was successful in his mission is beyond any question and doubt.

2

The Text

ॐ श्री गणेशाय नमः ।

सच्चिदानन्दमात्मानमद्वयाखण्डमच्युतम् ।
ध्यात्वा प्रश्नावली सम्यक् क्रियते मोक्षसिद्धये ॥

तत्र कान्यनुबंधानि[1] ।१। का प्रकृतिः[2] ।२। का माया ।३। का अविद्या ।४। कान्यपंचीकृतपंचभूतानि ।५। तेषां कथमुत्पत्तिः किं नामकानि च ।६। किं सूक्ष्मशरीरं ।७ ।कानि पंचीकृतपंचभूतानि ।८। कथं स्थूलशरीरोत्पत्तिः ।९। को ब्राह्मणो जीवो वा, जाति वा, पाण्डित्यं वा, वर्णो वा, कर्मो[3] वा, देहो वा ।१०। किं मूलाऽज्ञानं ।११। किं तुलाऽज्ञानं ।१२। किं[4] सोपाधिको भ्रमः ।१३। किं[5] निरुपाधिको भ्रमः ।१४। का प्रत्यभिज्ञा ।१५। कः भ्रमः ।१६। के प्रतिबंधाः[6] ।१७। तेषां निवृत्तिः कथं ।१८। को[7]

1. All the mss. incorporate the incorrect reading कान्यनुबन्धानि । Here the correct reading is के अनुबन्धाः ।
2. Mss. no. 2, 3 & 4 omit the affix (:) here.
3. कर्म is the correct reading.
4. Mss. 1, 2, 3 & 4 read किम् which should be कः ।
5. All the mss. except no. 4 read किं but the correct from is कः ।
6. Ms. no. 1 only shows the correct reading. All the other mss. read here तानि प्रतिबंधानि कानि ।
7. Mss. 2, 3 & 5 read किं ।

बंधः ।१९। कः[8] मोक्षः ।२०। कियंतो[9] ज्ञानानि ।२१। तेषां स्वरूपं किम् ।२२। कः[10] जीवः ।२३। तस्यार्थः किम् ।२४। कः[11] ईश्वरः ।२५। तस्यार्थः किं ।२६। के संशयाः ।२७। किं* विपर्ययः ।२८। किं ब्रह्म ।२९। किं तस्य स्वरूपम् ।३०। किं[12*] उपसत्तिः ।३१। किमेकपरत्वं* ।३२। किमनुभवार्थः ।३३। का लक्षणा वृत्तिः ।३४। किं* परिणामवादः ।३५। किमारंभवादः ।३६। किं* विवर्तवादः ।३७। कानि प्रमाणानि ।३८। किं* शिष्यार्थः ।३९। किं* गुरोरर्थः ।४०। किं तस्य लक्षणम् ।४१। किं*मात्मार्थः ।४२। किं* परमात्मार्थः ।४३। किं* संन्यासार्थः ।४४। किं* त्यागार्थः ।४५। किं* स्वरूपार्थः ।४६। किं* मकर्त्रर्थः ।४७। किं* वस्त्वर्थः ।४८। किं* चिदर्थः ।४९। कि*मानन्दार्थः ।५०। कि*मनंतार्थः ।५१। कि*मेकतार्थः ।५२। यदि शिष्यो मुमुक्षुरेतान् प्रश्नान् कृत्वा गुरोरग्रे विज्ञापयति तस्य गुरुराह।

"तस्मै[13] स विद्वानुपसन्नाय प्राहेति" (मु० १/२/१३) श्रुतेः

तत्र वेदान्तोपनिषद्यधिकारी विषयसम्बन्धं प्रयोजनानि[14] इति अनुबंधचतुष्टयम्। तत्र साधनचतुष्टयसम्पन्नः प्रमाताऽधिकारी; साधनानि नित्यानित्यवस्तुविवेकः इहामुत्रार्थफलभोगविरागः शमदमोपरतितितिक्षाश्रद्धासमाधानानि षट् मुमुक्षुत्वमिति।

---

8. Mss. 2, 3 & 5 include the incorrect reading किं।
9. Here the correct from should be कियन्ति।
10. Ms. no. 4 only presents the correct reading कः जीवः। Others read किं।
11. All the mss. except no. 4 read किं।
12. का is the correct reading here, but all the mss. present it as such.
13. Ms. no. 1 omit the Śruti.
14. All the mss. except no. 1 omit इति अनुबन्धचतुष्टयम्।

* In all the cases the correct reading should be कः but everywhere the texts read as such unanimously. The present reading however may be free from error, if the indeclinable इति be added at the end of each sentence.

It is curious to note here that ms. no. 5, omits several questions from Q. no. 46 up to no. 50.

जीवब्रह्मैक्यं वेदान्तानां विषयः; जीवब्रह्मैक्यबोध्यस्य बोधकोपनिषत् प्रमाणस्य बोध्यबोधकभाव संबंधः, जीवब्रह्मैक्य तद्गताऽनादिसांताऽज्ञाननिवृत्तिस्तदैक्यावाप्तिश्च प्रयोजनम् एवमेतान्यनुबंधानि[15]। अनादिसांता गुणानां साम्यावस्था प्रकृतिः। "ते ध्यानयोगानुगता[16] अपश्यन् देवात्मशक्तिं स्वगुणैर्निगूढां" (श्वेताश्व० १/३) "तम आसीदि" त्यादि (ऋ० १०/१२९/३) श्रुतेः।२। शुद्ध-सत्वप्रधाना सा ईश्वरोपाधिर्माया।३। मायायाः कतिपयांशैर्मलिनसत्वप्रधाना जीवोपाधिरविद्या; "माया[17] चाविद्या च स्वयमेव भवती"ति (नृसिंह ९) श्रुतेश्च।४। पृथक् पृथक्ऽपंचीकृतपंचभूतानि।५।"तस्माद्वा एतस्मादात्मन आकाशः सम्भूतः, आकाशाद्वायुर्वायोरग्निरग्नेरापो अद्भ्यः पृथिवी" (तै० २/१/३) चेत्यादि श्रुतेरेवं तेषामुत्पत्तिः। तन्मात्राण्यपंचीकृतानि सूक्ष्म-भूतान्येतन्नामकानि ।६। पूर्वोक्तेभ्योऽपंचीकृतपंचभूतेभ्यो[18] ज्ञानेन्द्रिय-पंचकं, कर्मेन्द्रिय पंचकं, प्राणपंचकं मनोबुद्धी अयमेव[19] त्रिकोशात्मकं सूक्ष्मशरीरम्।७। ईश्वरेच्छया पंचभूतानि द्विधा समाभवन्ति। तेषां मध्ये प्राथमिकान् पंचभागानेकमेकं चतुर्धा समं विभज्य तेषां चतुश्चतुर्भागानां स्वस्यार्धभागं परित्यागेन[20] भागान्तरेषु योजनमेतानि पंचीकृतपंचभूतानि।८। एतेभ्यः पंचीकृत पंचभूतेभ्यो ब्रह्माण्डस्तद्गतचतुर्दशभुवनानि चतुर्बिधं स्थूलशरीरं भोग्यान्नपानादिरुत्पत्तिर्भवति[21]। "पृथिव्या औषधय[22]

---

15. Here the correct reading should be एवमेते अनुबन्धाः, but all the mss. present the reading as such.

16. *Śvet. Up.*, 1/3 reads as follows:
"ते ध्यानयोगानुगता अपश्यन् देवात्मशक्तिं स्वगुणैर्निगूढाम्।"
Mss. no. 2, 3, 4 & 5 omit "ते ध्यान योगानुगता अपश्यन्" only ms. no. 1 quotes the entire line.

17. Ms. no. 5 reads "माया त्वाविद्या च स्वमेव भवति" which is incorrect.

18. Here mss. no. 2, 3, 4 & 5 omit the expected noun पंचभूतेभ्यः which is presented only in ms. no. 1.

19. To be grammatically correct it should read इदमेव।

20. Ms. no. 1 & 2 read परिभागेन which is not correct. The accepted reading however is not grammatically correct. It should read as स्वार्धभागपरित्यागेन or परित्यज्य in place of परित्यागेन।

21. After अन्नपानादि, इत्येषाम् should be incorporated to make the sentence correct.

22. All the mss. incorporate the reading औषधय औषधीभ्यो but *Taitt Up.*, 2/1/3 reads as "पृथिव्या ओषधय ओषधीभ्योऽन्नम्।"

औषधीभ्योऽन्नमन्नाद्रेतो रेतसो देह" (तै० २/१/३) इत्यादि श्रुतेः। इत्थं स्थूलशरीरोत्पत्तिः।९। जीवो ब्राह्मणश्चेत् [23]स यत्र कुत्र देहे उपलब्धत्वान्न जीवस्य ब्राह्मण्यम्।[24] जातिस्तु जडत्वान्न जातेर्ब्राह्मण्यम्। पाण्डित्यं ब्राह्मण्यंचेत्तर्हि शास्त्रार्थकर्तारो वहवः सन्ति, तस्मान्न पाण्डित्यं ब्राह्मण्यम्। ब्राह्मणः श्वेतवर्णः क्षत्रियो रक्तवर्णः वैश्यो पीतवर्णः शूद्रः श्यामवर्णः, अत्र नियमाभावान्न वर्णस्य ब्राह्मण्यम्। [25]कर्मणः कर्तारो वहवः सन्ति, तस्मान्न कर्मणो ब्राह्मण्यम्। देहो ब्राह्मणश्चेत् स तु त्वक्रक्तमांसमज्जास्थिवीर्यादिरूपत्वादतिव्याप्तिः स्यात् पुनर्देहो ब्राह्मणश्चेत्तर्हि पितुर्दाहक्रियायां पुत्रस्य ब्रह्महत्यायाः प्रसंगान्न देहस्य ब्राह्मण्यम्। तस्मात् कश्चित् पुण्यवशात् शुद्धान्तःकरणः साधनचतुष्टयसम्पन्नः सन् सन्न्यासानन्तरं विचारं कृत्वा वेदान्तस्य श्रवणादिना आत्मा ब्रह्मैव [C]साक्षात्कारो यस्य स एव ब्राह्मणः। तदुक्तं,

"जन्मना जायते शूद्रो संस्काराद्द्विज उच्यते।
वेद पाठाद्भवेद्विप्रो ब्रह्म जानाति ब्राह्मणः"[26] ॥१०॥

मूलः स्वतो जड़ः, स चैतन्यप्रकाशादाध्यासिकसंबंधात् प्रपंचस्य [27]कारणं "मयाध्यक्षेण[28] प्रकृतिः सूयते सचराचरमि"ति (गीता ९/१०) स्मृतेः "देवात्मशक्तिमि"ति (श्वेताश्व०

---

23. Here correct reading is तस्य।

24. जातेस्तु will be the correct form.

25. Only Ms. no. 1 shows here an additional word ब्राह्मणश्चेत् which makes the sentence as well as the sense incomplete therefore it has not been incorporated in the body of the text.

C. To make the sense correct the last part of the sentence should be constructed as follows:
"इति साक्षात्कारी भवति य स एव ब्राह्मणः।"

26. This verse is found in यतिधर्मसमुच्चय of विश्वेश्वर सरस्वती verse no. 50. A similar verse is found in *Atri-Saṁhitā*, verse no. 140.
"जन्मना ब्राह्मणो ज्ञेयः संस्काराद्द्विज उच्यते।
वेदपाठाद्भवेद्विप्रो श्रोत्रियस्त्रिभिरेव च॥"

27. Ms. no. 1 omits the word कारणं।

28. Ms. no. 3 reads मायाध्यक्षेण।

१/३)[29] श्रुतेरिदं मूलाऽज्ञानम् अथवा सर्व प्रपंचस्य दृश्यस्य द्रष्टाऽत्म-शक्तिद्वारानाद्यविनाशि अतिसूक्ष्मत्वाद्बीजवत् परमकारणं तस्य मूलस्याज्ञानं[30] मूलाऽज्ञानं ।११। घटाज्ञानं पटाज्ञानमित्यनुभवसिद्धत्वाद्विज्ञानिनामप्युपलभ्यमानत्वाद-किंचित्करमिति तुलाऽज्ञानं ।१२। यथा स्फटिकं शुद्धमपि ज्ञातं रक्तपुष्पादि समीपक[31]-संबंधाल्लोहितत्वद्भाति तद्वत् ज्ञानिना आत्मा शुद्धमपि ज्ञातं प्रारब्धवशाद्विश्वकर्तृत्वादि, अन्तःकरणसंबंधात् प्रपंचादिवद्भातीति सोपाधिको भ्रमः ।१३। शुक्ति[32] स्थाण्वादौ रजतपुरुषादेः केवलभ्रमकार्यत्वेन निरुपाधिकस्तद्वत् कर्तृत्वाद्यात्मनि वास्तवोऽज्ञानिनां दृश्यतेऽयं निरुपाधिको भ्रमः ।१४। यथार्थज्ञानं मूलं[33] यस्याः सा प्रत्यभिज्ञा[34]। यथा सोऽयं देवदत्तः,[35] सुखमहमस्वाप्सं, तत्त्वमस्यहं ब्रह्मास्मीति प्रत्यभिज्ञायते[36] इति प्रत्यभिज्ञा ।१५।

संस्कारमात्रजन्यं ज्ञानं स्मृतिः। सापि द्विविधा यथार्थाऽयथार्था च। यथार्था स्मृतिः द्विविधा, अनात्मस्मृतिरात्मस्मृतिश्च। तत्रायं प्रपंचो मिथ्या दृश्यत्वात् शुक्तिरूप्यवत्; एतस्य मिथ्यात्वानुसंधानं यथार्थाऽनात्मस्मृतिः तत्त्वमस्यादि वाक्यार्थानुसंधानं[37]

---

29. Mss. no. 2 & 5 present the reading श्रुतेरियं, whereas no. 1 & 4 read as श्रुतेरेवं।

30. It is curious to note here that except no. 5 all the four mss. read here तस्य मूलस्य ज्ञानं। This reading conveys the opposite sense, which is contradictory to the theory of Advaita Philosophy. Therefore the correct reading has been accepted in the text.

31. Ms. no. 1 omits समीपकं, Ms. no. 3 reads as समीप।

* Text 13 Language of the text here is cumbrous and grammatically incorrect. The correct reading should be as follows: "यथा स्फटिकं शुद्धं ज्ञातमपि रक्तपुष्पादि समीपक सम्बन्धाल्लोहितत्ववद्भाति तद्वत् ज्ञानिना आत्मा शुद्धतया ज्ञातोऽपि प्रारब्धवशात्तस्य विश्वकर्तृत्वादि अन्तःकरणसम्बन्धात् सप्रपंचादिवत् भातीति सोपाधिको भ्रमः।"

32. Only ms. no. 1 reads as शुक्तिकाः।

33. Mss. no. 2, 3, 4 & 5 read मूलो।

34. Ms. no. 3 reads here प्रतिभिज्ञा which is incorrect.

35. Ms. no. 3 reads देतः।

36. Ms. no. 3 omits प्रत्यभिज्ञायते इति प्रत्यभिज्ञा।

37. Ms. no. 3 reads the sentence as follows : "तत्त्वमस्यादि वाक्यार्थास्मृतिः।"

यथार्थात्मस्मृतिः। अयथार्था स्मृतिरपि द्विविधा अनात्मस्मृतिरात्मस्मृतिश्च। पूर्ववत् प्रपंचस्य सत्यत्वानुसंधानं अयथार्थाऽनात्मस्मृतिः,अहंकारादिष्वात्मत्वानुसंधानमात्मनि कर्तृत्वाद्यनुसंधानमयथार्थमात्मस्मृतिरयं भ्रमः।१६। प्रतिबंधस्त्रिबिधः, भूतभविष्य[38]-वर्तमानभेदात्। तत्र विचारात् संन्यासतश्च पूर्वंकस्यचिद्विषये याऽत्यंतप्रीतिः साऽज्ञानस्य भूतप्रतिबंधः। भावी प्रारब्धशेषवशात् शरीरातंरावाप्तिः, ब्रह्मलोकस्य प्राप्तिश्च भविष्यत् प्रतिबंधः। वर्तमानश्चतुर्बिधः, विचारकाले बिषयासक्तिश्च, बुद्धिमंदता, कुतर्कश्च, देहाद्यभिमाने आग्रहश्च। तदुक्तं,

"प्रतिबंधो वर्तमानो[39] विषयासक्तिलक्षणः।
प्रज्ञामान्द्यं[40] कुतर्कश्च विपर्ययः दुराग्रहः॥"

(पंच० ९/४३)

एतानि प्रतिबंधानि।१७। संवादि भ्रमान्निर्गुण ब्रह्मोपासनरूपात् कदाचित् साक्षात्कारात् भूतप्रतिबंधस्य निवृत्तिः। जन्ममात्राद्भबिष्यत् प्रतिबंधस्य निवृत्तिः। वैराग्यतश्च[41] श्रवणमननिदिध्यासनैरुपायैर्वर्तमानप्रतिबंधस्य निवृत्तिः। यदि कस्यचित् पुरुषस्य वेदान्तविचारादात्मसाक्षात्कारो भवेत्तर्हीयमेव परीक्षा कस्मादात्मसाक्षात्कारस्य प्रतिबंधरहितत्वात्[42] एव तेषां निवृत्तिः।१८। देहादावात्मवुद्धिरनाद्यविद्यायाः[43] सद्भावः स एव बंधः।१९। साधनसम्पन्नः सन् गुरुशास्त्रादात्मानात्मविवेकं[44] कृत्वाऽत्म-ब्रह्मसाक्षात्कारो भवति। "ब्रह्मैव सन् ब्रह्माप्येती"ति[45] (बृहदा० ४/४/६; नृसिंह/५) श्रुतेः, तस्मादात्मज्ञानादविद्याया[46] निवृत्तिरेव मोक्षः।२०। ज्ञानं द्विविधं, व्यवहारिकं

38. Mss. no. 2 & 4 read भविष्यत्।
39. Ms. no. 1 reads वर्तमान।
40. Ms. no. 3 & 5 read here प्रज्ञामन्द्यं, which is incorrect.
41. All the mss. except no. 4 read वैराग्यश्च।
42. Only Ms. no. 1 reads here प्रतिबन्धरहितत्वात्। Others however read प्रतिबन्धराहित्यत्वात्। The indeclinable एव finds no relevance here.
43. Mss. no. 2, 3, 4 & 5 present here the reading देहाद्यात्मबुद्धिः।
44. गुरुशास्त्राभ्यां is a better reading here.
45. Ms. no. 1 reads ब्रह्माण्येतीदीति, which is not correct.
46. In the Ms. no. 1 the reading is अविद्यया।

पारमार्थिकंचेति। तत्र व्यवहारिकं राजसतामसवृत्तिभेदात् घटज्ञानं पटज्ञानं देवतामूर्तिज्ञानम् ईश्वरज्ञानं शास्त्रीयज्ञानम् अन्तःकरणस्य विकाराण्यनतांनि। पारमार्थिकं त्वेकमेव शुद्धसत्वात्मबिषयमेवं ज्ञानानि।२१। घटज्ञानेन घटस्य साक्षात्कारः, पटज्ञानेन[47] पटस्य साक्षात्कारः एवमीश्वरादिपर्यतंस्य[48] कस्याश्चिद्‌देवतायाश्च साक्षात्कारः एवं तेषां स्वरूपः[49] ।२२।

एकमेवाज्ञानं विक्षेपशक्तिरावरणशक्तिरूपेण[50] मायाऽविद्ये[51]-त्युच्यते[52]। एतादृशाज्ञानोपहितचैतन्यं जीवेश्वरो जगच्च स्वयमेव भवति। "अजामेकां[53] लोहितशुक्लकृष्णां वह्वीः प्रजाः सृजमानां सरूपामि"ति (श्वेताश्व० ४/५) "देवात्मशक्तिमि"ति (श्वेताश्व० १/३) श्रुतेः। यथा स्वप्नगत[54] एक एव नृपो नानेव भवति, अयमेवैकजीववादः। केचित्तु समष्टिव्यष्टिरूपमज्ञानं स्वीकृत्य जीवेश्वरव्यवस्थां कुर्वन्ति। अस्मिंश्च पक्षेऽनेकजीववादः। केचित्तुं कारणीभूताज्ञानोपहितचैतन्यम्[55] ईश्वरः, कार्यरूपान्तःकरणोपहितो जीवः। अस्मिन्पक्षे आभासवादः प्रतिबिम्बवादो वा सम्भवति। तदुक्तं,

"यया यया भवेत् पुंसां व्युत्पत्तिः प्रत्यगात्मनि।
सा सैव प्रक्रिया ज्ञेया साध्वी सा च व्यवस्थिति"रिति॥
(पंच० ८/७३)

---

47. Ms. no. 1 omits here:
"पटज्ञानेन पटस्य साक्षात्कारः एवमीश्वरादि पर्यन्तस्य कस्याश्चिद्‌देवतायाश्च साक्षात्कारः।
48. Ms. no. 2 reads पर्यन्तेन।
49. स्वरूपम् is the correct form.
50. Ms. no. 2 reads रूप्येण।
51. Ms. no. 2 shows मायाऽविद्य।
52. The whole sentence should be constructed as follows: एकमेवाज्ञानं विक्षेपशक्त्यावरणशक्तिभेदेन मायाऽविद्या चेत्युच्यते।
53. Mss. 1 & 4 quote the entire line correctly while 2, 3 & 5 read अजामेकां and omit other words.
54. Ms. no. 2 shows the reading as "स्वपगत एव नृनानेव भवति।"
55. All the mss. except no. 1 show the reading चैतन्य।

तस्या[56] वस्थाभेदाद्विश्वतैजसप्राज्ञेत्युच्यते। जीवस्तु प्राणधारणादिति सर्वेषामविरोधादयं जीवः।२३। तस्य जीवस्यार्थौ द्विविधो वाच्यार्थौ लक्ष्यार्थश्च। पंचकोषसंयुक्तं चैतन्यमविविक्तं सद्वाच्यार्थः। अन्नमयः, प्राणमयः मनोमयो विज्ञानमय आनन्दमय एतेषां पंचकोषाणां मध्ये शरीराण्यप्यागतानि[57]। एतेभ्यः विविक्तं सल्लक्ष्यार्थः। एवं जीवस्य द्विबिधोऽर्थः।२४।

मायोपाधिकचैतन्यं[58] ईश्वरः। "मायां तु प्रकृतिं विद्यान्मायिनं तु महेश्वरमि"ति (श्वेताश्व० ४/१०) श्रुतेरयमीश्वरः। पूर्वोक्तेश्वरस्यार्थौ द्विविधः वाच्यार्थौ लक्ष्यार्थश्च। जगदुत्पत्तिस्थितिप्रलयस्थानं सदन्तर्यामित्वसर्वज्ञत्वसर्वेश्वरत्वादि-गुणसंयुक्तं चैतन्यमविविक्तं सद्वाच्यार्थः। विविक्तं सदखण्डचैतन्यं लक्ष्यार्थौ भवत्ययमीश्वरार्थः[59] ।२६। संशयास्त्रिबिधाः आत्मगत ईश्वरगत[60] ऐक्यगतश्चेति[61]। यथा स्थाणुर्वा, पुरुषो वा राक्षसो वा; तथाऽत्मा देहादिव्यतिरिक्तो वा न वा, व्यतिरिक्तत्वेऽपि कर्ता वा अकर्ता वा, अकर्तृत्वेऽपि चिद्रूपो वा न वा, चिद्रूपत्वेऽपि आनन्दात्मको वा नवेत्यात्मगतः ईश्वरोऽद्वितीयः सद्वितीयो वा अद्वितीयेऽपि आनन्दगुणको वा स्वरूपं वा आनन्दस्वरूपत्वेऽपि चिद्रूपो वा नवेति परमात्मगतः जीवस्य सच्चिदानन्दस्वरूपत्वेऽपि परमात्मना सहैक्यं भवति ऐक्येऽपि[62] तदज्ञानं मोक्षसाधनं न वा मोक्षसाधनत्वेऽपि तदज्ञानं[63] कर्मसमुच्चितं मोक्षसाधनं केवलज्ञानं वेत्यैक्यगतः, एते सर्वे संशया वेदान्त[64]-मननेनैव निवर्त्तन्ते।

---

56. Only Ms. no. 1 reads here तस्मात्।
57. Ms. no. 1 reads शरीरागतानि, no. 2 & 4 show शरीराण्यपगतानि, no. 3 presents शरीरास्प्यागतानि, while no. 5 only show the correct form.
58. Ms. no. 1 only reads the correct word चैतन्यम्।
59. Ms. no. 1 reads here: वृत्त्ययमीश्वरार्थः।
60. Here Ms. no. 2 shows the reading ईश्वगत।
61. Mss. no. 2 & 4 include the reading as एक्यगत।
62. Mss. no. 1, 2, 3 & 4 incorporate the incorrect reading एक्येपि।
63. Ms. no. 4 shows the dittography of the word ज्ञान। Perhaps this is a scribal mistake.
64. Ms. no. 1 reads here मननैव।

अवस्तुनि वस्तुबुद्धिः विपर्ययः, यथा असर्पवतिरज्वौ सर्पबुद्धिः,[65] तथाऽनात्मन्यात्म- बुद्धिर्विपर्ययः।२८। अखण्डैकरसो निरवयवोऽतएव सजातीयादि-भेदरहितो ब्रह्म। "एकमेवाद्वितीयं ब्रह्म" (छा० ६/२/१) "नेह नानास्ति किंचने[66]"ति (बृहदा० ४/४/१९) श्रुतेः। बृहत्त्वाद् ब्रह्म।२९। सच्चिदानन्दस्वरूपं "सत्यं ज्ञानमनन्तं ब्रह्मेति" (तै० २/१/१) "आनन्दो ब्रह्मे"त्यादि (तै० ३/६/१) श्रुत्याप्युक्तं[67] ब्रह्मस्वरूपम्।३०।

सम्प्रदायमार्गेण विश्वेश्वरीय वृत्त्यनुसारेण विधिपूर्वकं हंससन्न्यासादि मानस-सन्न्यासपर्यन्तं विधिपूर्वकं ब्रह्मनिष्ठा[68] दृगुरोरुपदेशं[69] गृह्यते सा उपसत्तिः।३१।

कस्यचिद्भाग्यमन्तो[70] ब्रह्मणश्चिन्तनादौ सुरुचिर्वर्धते[71] तदेकपरत्वं, यथापति-व्रतायाः पतिचिन्तनादौ रुचिर्भवति। तदुक्तं,

> "तच्चिन्तनं तत्कथनमन्योन्यं तत् प्रवोधने।
> एतदैक्य परत्वंच ब्रह्माभ्यासं विदुर्बुधाः" ॥
>
> (पंच० ७/१०६)

दीर्घकाल निरन्तरं सत्कारपूर्वकं वेदान्तस्य श्रवणमनननिदिध्यासनं ब्रह्मात्म-साक्षात्कारपर्यन्त पूर्वोक्तं यत् क्रियते[72] तदेकपरत्वम्।३२। उपसत्त्यादिना[73] श्रवणादेरनु[74] पश्चाद्भवेद् ब्रह्माहमस्मीत्यनुभवार्थः।३३।

---

65. Ms. no. 1 shows the reading सर्वबुद्धिः which is incorrect.
66. Mss. no. 2, 3 & 5 omit नेह नानास्ति किंचन। Only mss. no. 1 & 4 quote the entire line.
67. Ms. no. 4 reads आनन्दो ब्रह्मेति इत्याप्युक्तं, while ms. no. 5 shows the reading आनन्दो ब्रह्मेति इत्यादि श्रुत्याप्युक्त।
68. Ms. no. 1 shows the reading as ब्रह्मनिष्टा". . .
69. Here all the mss. incorporate the incorrect reading उपदेशं, but उपदेशः is a better reading here.
70. Ms. no. 1 shows the reading कस्यचिद्भाग्यवन्तो।
71. Ms. no. 2 reads here विवर्धते।
72. Mss. no. 1 & 4 read here कृयते, which is incorrect.
73. All the mss. read wrongly as उपसत्यादिना।
74. Ms. no. 1 reads श्रवणाहेतु।

लक्षणा त्रिविधाः जहल्लक्षणाऽजहल्लक्षणा जहदजहल्लक्षणा चेति। यथा [75]गङ्गायां घोषो वसतीति जहल्लक्षणा, सा तत्त्वमसीति वाक्ये न सम्भवति। यथा शोणो धावति वा मंचाः क्रोशन्तीत्यजहल्लक्षणापि तत्त्वमसीति[76] महावाक्ये न सङ्गच्छते। तस्मात् सोऽयं देवदत्त जहदजहल्लक्षणा तत्त्वमसीति महावाक्ये सम्भवति। तत्पदार्थे परोक्षत्वाद्यंशपरित्यागेन चिदंशोऽखण्डोऽवशिष्यते[77] त्वंपदार्थे[78] अपरोक्षत्वाद्यंश-परित्यागेन शुद्धं[79] कूटस्थचैतन्यमवशिष्यते। तत्त्वमसीति वाक्यस्याखण्डार्थोऽहं ब्रह्मास्मीति जहदजहल्लक्षणा वृत्तिः।३४। यथा दुग्धमेव दध्याकारं विपरिणमते, तथा प्रकृतिः प्रधानशब्दवाच्या मायैव जगदाकारं विपरिणामं गता। तथाहि माया सकाशान्महतत्त्वं महत्तत्वाद[80] हङ्कारोऽहङ्कारात् पंचमहाभूतानीत्यादिप्रक्रिया सांख्यानां मते परिणामवादः।३५।

यथा बहुमृत्कणिका[81]संमिलितो[82] घटो, यथा वा बहुतन्तुसंमिलितः पटस्तथा बहु अणु[83]संमिलितं जगदुत्पद्यते इति नैयायिकानां मते आरम्भवादः।३६। उपादानं त्रिविधं परिणामारंभविवर्त्तभेदात्। तत्र परिणामवादे स्वतो मायायाः परिणामो न सम्भवति देवात्मशक्तिमिति (श्वेताश्व० १/३) श्रुतिविरोधात् केवलायाः जड़त्वाच्च आरम्भ-वादेप्यणोर्निरवयवत्वस्वीकारात्तेषां संयोगायोगाद्वैचित्र्यं[84] न घटते। तस्माद्विवर्त्तोपादानं सम्भवति "परास्य शक्तिर्विविधैव श्रूयते स्वाभाविकीज्ञानवलक्रिया चेति" (श्वेताश्व० ६/८) श्रुतेः शक्तिद्वारा ब्रह्मैवोपादानं चिदंशेन निमित्तं चाऽज्ञानादि सर्वाऽनिर्वचनीयत्वेन मिथ्यात्वादद्वैतसिद्धिरभूत् अयमेव विवर्त्तवादः।३७। नैयायिकानां मते

---

75. Ms. no. 1 omits the sentence "यथा गंगायां घोषो वसतीति जहल्लक्षणा।"

76. Here ms. no. 4 contains an additional word सा।

77. Ms. no. 1 reads as चिदंशंमखण्डमवशिष्यते।

78. Ms. no. 1 reads as तत्त्वे।

79. Mss. no. 2, 3, 4 & 5 read here "शुद्धकूटस्थचैतन्योऽवशिष्यते।"

80. Ms. no. 2 omits here अहंकारो अहंकारात्।

81. Ms. no. 1 shows here the reading कणका।

82. Mss. no. 1 & 3 read संमिलतो।

83. Mss. no. 1 & 2 shows the reading अणुसम्मिलितं।

84. Ms. no. 3 contains additional reading here:

→

प्रत्यक्षानुमानोपमानशब्दाश्चत्वारः प्रमाणानि। वेदान्तमते प्रत्यक्षानुमानोपमान-शब्दार्थापत्त्यभावा षट् प्रमाणानि। पुराणमते षडेते चैतिह्य[85] सम्भवो च अष्ट प्रमाणानि। सर्वेषां शब्दप्रमाणं प्रवलम्। "तत्त्वमस्यहं ब्रह्मास्मी"त्यादि (छा० ६/८/७, बृहदा० १/४/१०) श्रुतिवाक्यानि प्रमाणानि।३८।

शिष्यः साधनसम्पन्नः सन् गुरुमनुसरति। तदुक्तं,

"प्रशान्तचित्ताय[86] जितेन्द्रियाय प्रहीणदोषाय यथोक्तकारिणे।
गुणान्वितायानुगताय सर्वदा प्रदेयमेतत् सततं मुमुक्षवे॥"
(*उप० सा०*, १६/७२)

वेदान्तस्याधिकारीति पूर्वमेवानुबन्धनिरूपणप्रसंगे निरूपितः[87] शिष्यार्थोऽयं शिष्यार्थः।३९। वेदस्य तात्पर्यार्थज्ञो ब्रह्मनिष्ठ आप्तोऽन्यस्य बोधनसामर्थ्यं यस्य गौरवलक्षणेन संयुक्तः स गुरुः। "समित्पाणिः श्रोत्रियं ब्रह्मनिष्ठं गुरुमुपगच्छेदि"-त्यादि (मु० १/२/१२) श्रुतेरयं गुरोरर्थः, यथा शीतादिहरणमग्नेरसाधारणं लक्षणं भवति।४०। यथा वा महद्रोगादिहरणं धात्वाद्यौषधस्यासाधारणलक्षणं भवति, तथा अनादिकालमारभ्य संसारतापत्रयसन्सप्तं[88] शरणागतं स्वशिष्यं ब्रह्मोपदेशेन शीतलं करोतीत्य-साधारणं गुरो[89]र्लक्षणम्। तदुक्तं,

"गुशब्दस्यान्धकारस्य रुशब्दस्तन्निरोधकः।
अन्धकारनिरुद्धत्वाद्गुरुरित्यभिधीयते॥" (*गुरुगीता*, १९)

इदं गुरोर्लक्षणम्।४१।

→ अस्येश्वरस्य शक्तिर्माया स्वकार्यापेक्षया परा विचित्रं कार्यकारित्वात् विविधा सा त्वैतिनिह्यमाजसिद्धानप्रमाणमात्रसिद्धेत्याह श्रूयत इति ज्ञानरूपेण वलेन या सृष्टिक्रियास्वाभाविक्यानादि मायात्मकत्वादित्यर्थः।

85. Ms. no. 3 contains this excess reading which is incorrect and illegible:

"चैतिह्य सांपूर्वावस्थामपरित्यज्यावस्थान्तरायति लक्षणो विवर्त्तोपादानत्वभव च।"

86. Ms. no. 1 shows यतेन्द्रियाय।

87. निरूपितशिष्यार्थः is seen in ms. no. 1.

88. Ms. no. 2 reads तप्तं।

89. Mss. no. 3, 4 & 5 read असाधारणगुरोः।

अततीत्यात्मा यथा वा स्वमात्मैवात्माकूटस्थोऽकर्त्तादेहाद्यहंकारादेर्जडस्य साक्षी। "असंगोह्ययं पुरुषः" (बृहदा० ४/३/१५) इति श्रुति"रयमात्मा सर्वस्यान्तर" (बृहदा० ३/५/१) इति च श्रुतिः प्रसिद्धा। अयमात्मा सर्वान्तरो भवितुर्महति सर्वस्य साक्षित्वाच्च स्वसभायां[90]नृपवत्। "असंगोऽहं" निर्विकारोऽहमिति विद्वदनुभवोऽप्यस्त्ययमात्मार्थः।४२। स एव परमात्मा परमो देहादिभ्य उत्कृष्ट आत्मा परमात्मा जीवस्य बुद्धौ चित्प्रतिबिम्बस्य निजं रूपं लक्ष्यार्थ[91] मित्यर्थः। "एष इन्द्रः एष वरुणः एष सर्वेश्वर" इत्यादि (मा० ४/४/६) "तस्य[92] भासा सर्वमिदं विभाती"त्यादि (मु० २/२/१०, कठ० २/१/१५, श्वेताश्व० ६/१४) श्रुतेरयं परमात्मार्थः।४३।

संन्यासश्चतुर्विधः। तीव्रवैराग्ययुक्तस्य कुटीचरो[93] बहूदको[94] वा संन्यासः शास्त्रेणोच्यते। तीव्रवैराग्ययुक्तस्यात्माना[95]त्मविवेकरूपो विधिपूर्वको हंससंन्यास इत्यभिधीयते। शास्त्रे परवैराग्ययुक्तस्य[96] ब्रह्मज्ञानोत्तरकाले विधिना शिखासूत्रादित्यागरूपः परमहंससंन्यासोऽयमेव विद्वत् संन्यास इत्युच्यते। यथायोग्योऽयं संन्यासार्थः।

"सर्वकर्माणि मनसा संन्यस्यास्ते सुखं वशी।
नवद्वारे पुरे देही नैव कुर्वन्न कारयन्नि"ति॥

(*गीता*० ५/१३)

श्रीमद्भगवद्वचनात् "ब्रह्मचर्यादेव व्रजेत् गृहस्थादेव प्रव्रजेद्वानप्रस्थादेवे"त्यादि (जाबाल० ४) श्रुतेः। सम्यक् प्रकारेण कर्मणां न्यासः संन्यासोऽयं संन्यासार्थः।४४।

---

90. Ms. no. 2 reads सभायं नृपवत्।
91. Variants — लक्ष्यार्थ and चक्षार्थः।
92. Mss. read यस्य here.
93. Variants कुटस्थक in ms. 1. कुटीचक in Mss. 3, 4 & 5.
94. Mss. read बहुदकः।
95. Ms. no. 2 omits "आत्मानात्मविवेकरूपविधिपूर्वको हंससन्न्यास इत्यभिधीयते।
96. Ms. no. 1 reads परं वैराग्ययुक्तस्य।

त्यागो हि द्विविधः। कर्मफलत्यागो दृश्यत्यागश्चेति।
फलत्यागः[97] — श्रीभगवतोक्तं गीतायां[98],

"अनाश्रितः कर्मफलं कार्यं कर्म करोति यः
स संन्यासी च योगी च न निरग्निर्न चाक्रियः॥"
(*गीता०* ६/१)

इत्यविद्वांसं प्रति कर्मफलत्यागस्य स्तुत्वोपदिष्टम्।
दृश्यत्यागः[99] श्रीमुनिमाधवानन्दगुरुणोक्तत्वात् शृणु,

"ब्रह्मैवाहं त्रिगुणरहितं पंच[100]पाशैर्विमुक्तं
षड्भावैश्च षडूर्मिभिर्विरहितं शुद्धं प्रपंचात् परं[101]
ब्रह्माविष्णु महेश्वराश्च जगति जीवत्वं नानाविधा[102]
नो जाने क्व गता ममैव परमज्ञानोदये स्वप्नवत्॥"

कार्येण सह अज्ञानरूपस्य त्यागः[103] ब्रह्मात्मज्ञानिनां[104] विद्यतेऽयं त्यागार्थः ।४५।
स्व[105] स्वरूपः स्वरूप आत्मशब्देन लक्ष्यते यस्मिन्नात्मन्यध्यस्तानि देहेन्द्रियप्राणान्तः-

---

97. Ms. no. 4 omits here from:
फलत्यागः — श्री भगवतोक्तं गीतायां
"अनाश्रितः कर्मफलं कार्यं कर्म करोति यः।
स सन्न्यासी च योगी च ननिरग्निर्नचाक्रियः"॥ इत्यविद्वांसं प्रति।

98. Variants: श्री श्रीगीतायां in mss. 1 & 4, गीतासु in ms. no. 2.

99. All the mss., except no. 4 reads दृश्यत्यागं।

100. Only ms. no. 3 contains additional reading:
"अस्तिजायत्येदिछुदापीपाशाशोकमोहजारामृत्युविअद्याऽस्मदारागद्वेषअभिनिवेस।"

101. Ms. no. 5 reads प्रपंचात् परो।

102. Variant reading: नानाभिधा is seen in mss. no. 2, 4 & 5.

103. All the mss. except no. 4 read as त्यागं।

104. Ms. no. 1 only shows the additional reading: देहेन्द्रियप्राणान्तः before विद्यते।

105. Here the correct reading should be as follows:
"स्वः स्वरूपं स्वरूपमात्मशब्देन लक्ष्यते यस्मिस्न्नात्मन्यध्यस्तानि देहेन्द्रिय प्राणान्तःकरणादीन्यपि आत्मशब्दे प्रवर्त्तते। But all the mss. present it as such which appears to be incorrect.

करणादीनामप्यात्मशब्दः प्रवर्तते स प्रत्यगात्मा। "एष स आत्मा सर्वस्यान्तर" (बृहदा० ३/५/१) इति श्रुतेरयं स्वरूपार्थः।४६। स एवात्माऽकर्ता। तदुक्तं,

"यस्य नाहंकृतो भावो बुद्धिर्यस्य न लिप्यते
हत्वापि स इमाँल्लोकान्न हन्ति न निबध्यते॥
(*गीता*० १८/१७)

"प्रकृत्यैव च कर्माणि क्रियमाणानि सर्वशः।
यः पश्यति तथात्मानम कर्तारं स पश्यति"॥
(*गीता*० १३/२९)

"असंगोह्ययं पुरुष" इति (*बृहदा*० ४/३/५) श्रुतेरयमकर्त्रार्थः[106]।४७। वस्तु कालत्रयावाध्यं[107] स एवात्मा साक्षी। तदुक्तं,

"सत्यत्वं बाधराहित्यं[108] जगद्बाधैक साक्षिणः।
बाधः किं साक्षि[109] को ब्रूहि[110] न त्वसाक्षिक[111] इष्यते[112]"॥
(*पंच*० ३/२९)

"सत्यं [113]ज्ञानमनन्तं ब्रह्म" (तै० २/१/१, सर्वोप० सा० शा०), "यत् सत्यं स आत्मा" (छा० ६/८/३, ६/४/४) "सदेव सोम्येदमग्र आसीदेकमेवाद्वितीयं ब्रह्मे"त्यादि (छा० ६/२/१) नित्यंच सत्यंचैकमेव स एव वस्त्वर्थः।४८। चित् स्वप्रकाशो यस्तूर्यावस्था[114]

---

106. Here the correct reading should be अकर्त्रर्थ but all the mss. incorporate the reading as such.
107. Ms. no. 3 reads here incorrectly त्रयावाध्व।
108. Here ms. no. 3 incorporates the reading वाधराहत्यं।
109. Ms. no. 3 reads here साक्षको, whereas no. 5 shows साज्ञको।
110. Ms. no. 4 reads here ब्रूहे।
111. Ms. no. 3 shows the reading साक्षाक।
112. Mss. no. 3 & 5 read here इक्षते।
113. Ms. no. 3 reads incorrectly ग्यानम्।
114. All the mss. except no. 4 show different incorrect readings here like (1) प्रक्रियावस्था, (2) यस्त्वयावस्था, (3 & 5) यस्त्रयावस्था।

साक्ष्यऽन्वयव्यतिरेकाभ्यां स्वतःसिद्धोऽखंडचैतन्यः "अत्रायं पुरुषः स्वयंज्योतिर्भवति" (बृहदा० ४/३/९) "तस्य[115] भासा सर्वमिदं विभाती"त्यादि (*कठ०* २/१/१५, *मु०* २/२/१०, *श्वेताश्व०* ६/१४) श्रुतेरयं चिदर्थः[116]।४९।

आनन्दः परमप्रेमास्पदं[117] स्वकं[118] रूपं भवति। तदुक्तं,

"परप्रेमास्पदत्वेन[119] परमानन्दरूपता[120]।
सुखवृद्धि[121] प्रीति वृद्धौ सार्वभौमादिषु[122] श्रुता" ॥**

बृहदारण्यके याज्ञवल्क्यो मैत्रेयीं प्रत्युवाच; "न वा अरे पुत्रकामाय पुत्रो प्रियो भवति, आत्मनस्तु कामाय पुत्रः प्रियो भवती"त्यादिना "[123]न वा अरे सर्वं प्रियं भवति, आत्मनस्तु कामाय सर्वं प्रियं भवती"त्यन्तेन (*बृहदा०* ४/५/६), अन्यच्च "आनन्दो

---

115. All the mss. read this *śruti* incorrectly "यस्य भासा।"

116. Ms. no. 5 reads here चिदार्थः।

117. Ms. no. 1 reads परप्रेमास्पदं, no. 5 omits the sign (") and reads परप्रेमास्पद, whereas no. 3 shows the reading प्रमप्रेमास्पदं which is incorrect.

118. Ms. no. 1 show the reading स्वविरूपं।

119. Ms. no. 3 reads प्रमप्रेमास्पदत्वेन।

120. Ms. no. 3 shows the reading प्रमानन्दस्वरूपता, ms. no. 2 reads परमानन्दरूपताः, whereas no. 1 shows परमानन्दस्वरूपता।

121. Here the correct reading showed by सुखवृद्धिः, but all the mss. present it as such.

122. Ms. no. 1 reads here सार्वभौमादिसुश्रुताः, no. 3 reads सार्वभौमादिकुश्रुतेः, whereas no. 5 shows सार्वभौमादिक श्रुतेः।

** A similar verse is found in *Pañcadaśī* 12/72, with slight difference in reading.

"परप्रेमास्पदत्वेन परमानन्द इष्यताम्।
सुखवृद्धिः प्रीतिवृद्धौ सार्वभौमादिषु श्रुता॥"

123. Ms. no. 1 omits here the line from "न वा अरे पुत्रकामाय पुत्रो प्रियो भवति आत्मनस्तु कामाय पुत्रः प्रियो भवति . . . ।

ब्रह्म" "आनन्दाद्ध्येव[124] खल्विमानि भूतानि जायन्ते, आनन्देन जातानि जीवन्ति आनन्दं [125]प्रयान्त्यभिसंविशन्ति" (*तै०* ३/६) ब्रह्मपुच्छ[126] प्रतिष्ठेत्यादि (*तै०* २/५) श्रुतियुक्तिभ्यामानन्दस्वरूपं साधितं सच्चिदानन्दोऽस्मीति विद्वदनुभवाच्चाय-मानन्दार्थः।५०। देशकालवस्तुपरिच्छेदशून्यत्वमनन्तत्वम्[127] अथवा सजातीय-विजातीय[128] स्वगतभेदशून्यत्वमनन्तत्वम्। सर्वत्रव्यापकत्वाद्देशपरिच्छेद शून्यः नित्यत्वात् कालपरिच्छेदशून्यः सर्वात्मकत्वाद्वस्तुपरिच्छेदशून्यः, जडवर्गाद्[129] भिन्नं चैतन्यमेकमेव। तस्माज्जीवेश्वरयोर्न सजातीय-भेदः, चिद्रूपाद्विश्वस्य नानारूपत्वेना-वस्तुत्वान्नविजातीयभेदः, ब्रह्मात्मैकरसत्वान्निरवयवत्वाच्च न स्वगतभेदः। "विष्टभ्याहमिदं कृत्स्नमेकांशेन स्थितो जगदि"ति (*गीता०* १०/४२) स्मृतेः "पादोऽस्य विश्वा[130] भूतानि त्रिपादस्ति[131] स्वयंप्रभः" (*छा०* ३/१२/६, *पु० सू०* ३), "सत्यं ज्ञानमनन्तं ब्रह्मे"त्यादि (*तै०* २/१/१, *सर्वोप० सा० शा०* १०) श्रुतेरयमनन्तार्थः।५१।

जहदजहल्लक्षणया[132] जीवेश्वरयोरेकत्वमेकतार्थः। यथा सोऽयं देवदत्त इति वाक्ये तत्कालविशिष्टदेवदत्तस्य सशब्दार्थस्य एतत्कालविशिष्टदेवदत्तस्यायं शब्दार्थस्य च

---

124. Here all the mss. show different incorrect readings like, (1 & 4) आनन्दादेव खल्विमानि भूतानि जायते (2 & 3) आनन्दादेव . . . & (5) shows: आनन्दाथेव but *Taitt. Up.*, 3/6 reads आनन्दाद्ध्येव खल्विमानि भूतानि जायन्ते . . .

125. Here all the mss. show different incorrect readings:
(1) प्रत्यभिसंविशन्ति, (2, 4, 5) प्रयान्त्यभिसंविशन्ति and (3) प्रत्ययान्त्यभिसंति But *Taitt. Up.*, 3/6 reads: आनन्दं प्रयन्त्यभिसंविशन्ति

126. All the mss. read incorrectly ब्रह्मपुच्छ प्रतिष्ठा but *Taitt. Up.*, 2/5 reads ब्रह्मपुच्छं प्रतिष्ठा।

127. Here ms. no. 1 reads आथवा।

128. Ms. no. 3 reads here वीजीतीय।

129. Mss. no. 2, 3 & 5 read भिन्नचैतन्यम् which is not correct.

130. This is quoted from *Chān*. However the printed editions of *Chān*. read सर्वा instead of विश्वा।

131. All the mss. except no. 1 incorporate the incorrect reading त्रिपादोस्ति।

132. Only ms. no. 1 reads here जहदजहल्लक्षणयो।

विरुद्ध[133] तत्कालैतत्कालविशिष्टांशपरित्यागेनाविरुद्धमेकमेव देवदत्तं लक्षयति। तथा च तत्त्वमसीति महावाक्येऽपि परोक्षत्वादिविशिष्टचैतन्यस्य तत्पदार्थस्यापरोक्षत्वादि-विशिष्टचैतन्यस्य त्वंपदार्थस्य च विरुद्ध[134] परोक्षत्वापरोक्षत्वादिविशिष्टांशपरित्यागेना-विरुद्धमेकमेव ब्रह्मचैतन्यं लक्षयति। तथा च सति जीवेश्वरयोरौपाधिको भेदः, न वास्तवो भेदः। तदुक्तं,

> "कूटस्थ[135] ब्रह्मणोर्भेदो नाममात्रादृते[136] न हि।
> घटाकाशमहाकाशौ वियुज्येते न हि क्वचित्" ॥
>
> (पंच० ६/२३७)

एतस्याभिप्रायः कथ्यते, यथैक एवाकाशश्चतुर्विधः,[137] मेघाकाशो, घटाकाशो जलाकाशो महाकाशश्चेति,[138] घटे जलं विद्यते तत्र य[139] आकाशस्य प्रतिबिम्बः स जलाकाशः तत्र मेघाकाशजलाकाशयोश्च त्यागे सत्यपि विवेकिनो घटाकाशमहाकाशयोरेकत्वमेव भासते। तथा एकमेव चैतन्यं[140] चतुर्विधं (१) मायोपाधिक ईश्वरः, (२) कूटस्थः, (३) चिदाभासो जीवः, (४) अखण्डसच्चिदानन्दश्च। तत्रेश्वरजीवयोश्च त्यागे सति विद्वद्भिः[141] कूटस्थचैतन्याखंडसच्चिदानन्दयोरेकत्वमेव भासते, अहमस्मि अनुभवामि, कदाचिदप्रियो न भवाम्येवमात्मा सच्चिदानन्दो[142] जीवस्य लक्ष्यार्थः, स एवेश्वरस्य लक्ष्यार्थः, सच्चिदानन्दः स एव ब्रह्माहमस्मीति[143] ज्ञातव्यः, एतद् ज्ञात्वा मर्त्योऽमृतो भवति।

---

133. All the mss. read incorrectly विरुद्धम्।
134. Mss. no. 1, 3, 4 & 5 read विरुद्धं, which is incorrect.
135. Mss. no. 1, 2, 3 & 5 present here the reading कूटस्थं which is erroneous.
136. Here all the mss. except no. 1 read नाममात्रादनेन हि।
137. Ms. no. 1 reads as यथैक एव आकाशश्चतुर्विधः, ms. no. 2 shows the reading यथा एक एवाकाशश्चतुर्विधः।
138. Here ms. no. 1 incorporates the reading as: महाकाशाश्चेति।
139. Here ms. no. 1 reads तत्रायं काशस्य, Ms. no. 2 shows तत्राकाशस्य।
140. Mss. no. 2, 3, 4 & 5 incorporate the reading चैतन्यश्चतुर्विधः।
141. Here the correct reading should be विदुषाम्।
142. Ms. no. 1 reads सच्चिदानन्द स, etc.
143. Ms. no. 1 drops here a letter and presents the reading ब्रह्माऽस्मीति।

यथा नेत्रं[144] दर्पणे स्वकं रूपं स्वयमेव लक्षयति [145]तथा आत्मापि शुद्धबुद्धौ [146]स्वकमखंडं सच्चिदानन्दस्वरूपं स्वयमेव लक्षयति। अहंवृत्तिविषयोह्यात्माऽयमेव साक्षात्कारोऽनुभवो विज्ञानंच,[147] इदमेव[148] विज्ञानं यस्यास्ति स कृतार्थो भवति, संचितानि कर्माण्यपि नाशं प्राप्नुवन्त्यागामिकर्माण्यपि न स्पृशन्ति, अकर्ताऽत्मज्ञानित्वात् ब्रह्मात्मज्ञानेन मूल्याऽज्ञानं[149] नाशयित्वात्मज्ञानाग्निना [150]वासनाः सर्वाः भर्जिताः। प्रारब्ध- वशाद्देहेन्द्रियान्तःकरण[151] प्राणादिषु क्रियां पश्यन् जीवन्मुक्तः सन् तिष्ठति। प्रारब्धकर्मपूर्णानन्तरमखंडसच्चिदानन्दस्वरूपेणावतिष्ठते या मतिः सागतिर्भवेदिति वचनात्।[152] अस्मिन्नेकतार्थे श्रुतिस्मृतीतिहासपुराणानि प्रमाणानि।[153]

"एको देवो सर्वभूतेषु गूढः सर्वव्यापी सर्वभूतान्तरात्मा।
कर्माध्यक्षः सर्वभूताधिवासः साक्षी चेता केवलो निर्गुणश्च॥"
(*श्वेताश्व*० ६/११)

"एकमेवाद्वितीयं ब्रह्म" (छा० ६/२/१) "नेह नानास्ति किंचन" (*बृहदा*० ४/४/१९) "तत्त्वमसि" (*छा*० ६/८/७, ६/९/४, ६/१०/३, ६/११/३, ६/१२/३, ६/१३/३, ६/१४/३, ६/१५/३, ६/१६/३), "अहं ब्रह्मास्मि" (*बृहदा*० १/४/१०) "ज्ञात्वा देवं मुच्यते सर्वपाशैः" (*श्वेताश्व*० १/८, २/१५, ४/१६, ४/१३, ६/१३), "तस्य तावदेव चिरं

---

144. Only ms. no. 1 reads here नेत्रे दर्पणे।
145. Here ms. no. 3 omits the entire sentence तथा आत्मापि शुद्धबुद्धौ स्वकमखण्डं सच्चिदानन्दस्वरूपं स्वयमेव लक्षयति।
146. Here mss. no. 4 & 5 reads as : स्वकमखण्डसच्चिदानन्दः।
147. Mss. no. 1, 2 & 5 read विज्ञानंच, no. 3 reads विज्ञानंश्च, while no. 4 reads विज्ञानश्च।
148. Ms. no. 1 reads here अयमेव विज्ञानं।
149. Mss. no. 1, 2 & 4 reads here मूलाज्ञानं।
150. Only ms. no. 1 reads वासनानि सर्वाणि भर्जतानि। The term भर्जतानि is an incorrect formation.
151. Ms. no. 2 incorporates the reading प्रमाणादिषु।
152. Ms. no. 1 includes here the reading वचनमनुसृत्य।
153. Ms. no. 2 omits the word प्रमाणानि।

यावन्न विमोक्ष्ये" (*छा०* ६/१४/२), "विमुक्तश्च विमुच्यते" (*कठ०* ४/२) इत्यादि श्रुतेः।

क्षेत्रज्ञंचापि मां विद्धि सर्वक्षेत्रेषु भारत।
क्षेत्रक्षेत्रज्ञयोर्ज्ञानं यत्तद्ज्ञानं[154] मतं मम॥
(*गीता०* १३/२)

यथा सर्वगतं सौक्ष्म्यादाकाशं[155] नोपलिप्यते।
सर्वत्रावस्थितो देहे तथात्मा नोपलिप्यते॥
(*गीता०* १३/३२)

यथा प्रकाशयत्येकः कृत्स्नं लोकमिमं रविः।
क्षेत्रं[156] क्षेत्री तथा कृत्स्नं प्रकाशयति भारत"॥
(*गीता०* १३/३३)

"आत्मानं विन्दते[157] यस्तु सर्वभूतगुहाशयम्।[158]
श्लोकेन यदिवाऽर्द्धेन क्षीणं तस्य प्रयोजनम्"॥
"ज्योतिरूपमरूपंच स्वरूपं हृदि संस्थितम्।
सर्वज्ञं[159] सर्वभूतस्थं सर्वेशं[160] सर्वतो मुखम्"॥

अखंडात्मासच्चिदानन्दः[161] ब्रह्म स एवाद्वैतात्मा इति एकतार्थः।५२। एवमात्मानं ज्ञात्वा कृतार्थोऽसीति।

---

154. Here all the mss. incorporate various incorrect readings like (1) यत्तु ज्ञानं मतं मम while 2, 3, 4 & 5 read as यत्तद् ज्ञानं मतं मम The actual verse shows the reading यत्तज् ज्ञानं मतं मम।

155. Ms. 5 shows here a scribal mistake सैक्ष्म्यादाकाशं।

156. Mss. no. 1 & 2 read: क्षेत्रक्षेत्री।

157. Mss. no. 1 & 3 present the reading as विद्यते।

158. Ms. no. 1 shows the reading सर्वभूतगूढ़ायाम्।

159. Ms. no. 1 only contains here an additional स।

160. Ms.no. 1 reads सर्वशः & no. 2 reads सर्वशंः।

161. Mss. no. 2 and 3 incorporate the reading as अखण्डात्मसच्चिदानन्दः।

3

English Translation

OBEISANCE to lord Gaṇeśa. Having meditated over the self, which is the existence (*sat*), consciousness (*cit*) and bliss (*ānanda*) as such, secondless (*advaya*), indivisible (*akhaṇḍa*) and infallible (*acyuta*) the series of questions, is put forth, for the proper attainment of the liberation.

However, **(1)** Which are to be meant by the term *anubandha* (preliminaries)? **(2)** What is *prakṛti* (primordial substance)? **(3)** What is *māyā*? **(4)** What is *avidyā*? **(5)** Which are *apañcīkṛtapañca-bhūtāni* (the non-quintuplicated five elements)? **(6)** How are they brought forth? What are their names? **(7)** What is (called) the subtle-body? **(8)** Which are *pañcīkṛtapañca-bhūtāni* (the quintuplicated five elements? **(9)** How did the gross bodies come into being? **(10)** Who is a brāhmaṇa? Does it refer to a being or a caste or the scholarship or the colour or the action or the body? **(11)** What is *mūla-ājñānam* (the primal nescience)? **(12)** What is *tulājñānam* (the secondary nescience)? **(13)** What is to be meant by the term *sopādhika bhrama* (attributive delusion)? **(14)** What is *nirupādhika bhrama* (the delusion without adjunct)? **(15)** What is (referred to here by the term) *pratyabhijñā* (recognition)? **(16)** What is illusion? **(17)** Which are *pratibandha*s (the impediments)? **(18)** How can they be removed? **(19)** What is *bandha* (a bondage)? **(20)** What is *mokṣa* (Liberation)? **(21)** How many types of knowledge are there? **(22)** What is their nature? **(23)** Who is *jīva* (a soul)? **(24)** What is referred to here by it (*jīva*)? **(25)** Who is *īśvara* (the highest soul)? **(26)** What is meant by "Him"? **(27)** How many types of *saṁśaya* (doubts) are there? **(28)** What is meant by *viparyaya* (misapprehension)?

(29) What is *Brahman*? **(30)** What is its exact nature? **(31)** What is (to be meant by the term) *upasatti* (approach)? **(32)** What is (meant by) *ekaparatva* (one pointed concentration)? **(33)** What is (meant by) *anubhava* (transcendental realization)? **(34)** What is implication? **(35)** What is (called) *pariṇāmavāda* (the theory of evolution)? **(36)** What is the *ārambhavāda* (the theory of origination)? **(37)** What is *vivartavāda* (the theory of phenomenal appearance)? **(38)** What are the means of valid knowledge? **(39)** Who is referred by the term *śiṣya* (the disciple)? **(40)** Who is meant by the word *guru* (the preceptor)? **(41)** Which is its defining characteristic? **(42)** What is the meaning of the term *ātman* (self)? **(43)** What is the meaning of the word *paramātman* (the highest self)? **(44)** What is meant by *saṁnyāsa* (renunciation)? **(45)** What is meant by *tyāga* (relinquishment)? **(46)** What is meant by essential nature (of the self)? **(47)** What is implied by the term *akartā* (non-agent)? **(48)** What is meant by *vastu* (the object)? **(49)** Which is meant by *cit* (consciousness)? **(50)** What is known by the term *ānanda* (bliss)? **(51)** What is the import of *ananta* (infinity)? **(52)** What is the import of the word *ekatā* (identification)?

If the disciple, having an yearning for liberation, prepares the questions and presents them to the preceptor, the preceptor instructs for him. This is supported by *śruti*: *tasmai savidvānupasannāya prāha* (*Muṇḍ.*, 1/2/13). (He speaks to that disciple, who has approached him duly.)

However, the four preliminaries are (1) the eligible student for the study of Vedānta and Upaniṣads, (2) the subject-matter, (3) the relation and (4) the necessity. The eligible student is the knower, enriched with the four means (*sādhana-catuṣṭaya-sampanna*) of attainment. The (so-called) means are (1) the discrimination between the permanent and transitory objects (*nityānityavastuvivekaḥ*), renunciation of the enjoyment of the result of the actions in this world and the world here after (*ihāmutrārthaphalabhoga-virāgaḥ*), (3) restraining of the outgoing mental propensities (*śama*), controlling over the external sense-organs (*dama*), withdrawing of the self (*uparati*), for-bearance (*titikṣā*), faith (*śraddhā*), and the self-settledness (*samādhāna*), these six and the state of yearning for the attainment of salvation. The subject-matter of Vedānta is the identification of the individual self with *Brahman*. Relation here means the relation of the implier and the implied between Upaniṣads playing the part of the means of knowledge and their import of unity of *jīva* and *brahma*. Necessity is the removal of the nescience, beginningless and having an end relating to the oneness of *jīva* and *brahma* and the attainment of that oneness. These are the four preliminary questions (explained here). **(1)** *Prakṛti* or primordial substance is the state of equilibrium of the *guṇas*, having an end but no beginning. This is known from the *śruti* texts like — *te dhyānayogānūgatā apaśyan devātma-śaktiṁ svaguṇairniguḍhāṁ* (Those who accepted the path of meditation, witnessed the power of illuminating self-suppressed by their *guṇas*) (*Śvet.* 1/3) *'tama āsīd' ityādi* (there was darkness, etc.) (*ṚV*, 10/129/3). **(2)** This *prakṛti*, when purified by *sattva* elements, is *māyā*, — an adjunct to *īśvara*. **(3)** This *sattva*, relating to *māyā*, being impured to some extent, becomes *avidyā* — an adjunct to *jīvas*. Thus says the *śruti* — *māyā cāvidyā ca svayameva bhavatīti* (*NṚST*, 9). (*Māyā*, as well as *avidyā* evolve spontaneously) **(4)**

(At first) there existed the uncompounded five elements separately. **(5)** Such is seen in the *śruti* — *tasmādvā etasmādātmana ākāśaḥ sambhūta, ākāśādvāyur vāyoragniragnerāpo adbhyaḥ pṛthivī cetyādi.* (From this self evolved *ākāśa*, from *ākāśa* came out *vāyu*, from *vāyu* came out fire, the water sprang out from fire and the earth from the water) (*Taitt.*, 2/1/3); thus they came into being. These uncompounded rudimentary elements are the subtle bodies, (they are) named as such (ether, air, fire, water and earth). **(6)** From these afore-said non-quintuplicated five elements came out the five sense-organs, the five organs of action, five vital forces, the mind and the intelligence; each of them is what is known as the subtle body consisting three cells. **(7)** By god's grace the five elements are divided into two equal halves. (Out of these ten parts) the first halves of each element are again sub-divided into four equal parts. Then leaving one half of each element, to the other half is added one of these quarters of the remaining four elements. In this way five elements are quintuplicated. **(8)** From these are created the cosmos including the fourteen world, four types of gross bodies and entertainments like food-drinks, etc. The *śruti* says — *pṛthivyā auṣadhaya, auṣadhībhyonnamannādreto retaso deha*. (The plants came out from the earth, from these herbs evolved food, the sperm came out from the food and the body is composed of the sperm) (*Taitt*., 2/1/3), thus the gross bodies are created. **(9)**

The being cannot be called a Brāhmaṇa because it is felt in every body at random. The caste being inanimate cannot be taken as Brāhmaṇa, nor the scholarship can be accepted as Brāhmaṇa because there are so many authors of the texts. (Let it be taken for granted) Brāhmaṇas are white, kṣatriyas are red, vaiśyas are yellow and śūdras are black, but no caste can be determined on the basis of colour. There are numerous agents of sacrificial rites and therefore Brāhmaṇahood cannot rest upon the mere activities. Let therefore body be the mark of Brāhmaṇa; but that is merely a composite of the skin, blood, flesh, bones, marrow and sperm and therefore the fault of over-applicability will occur. Moreover, if human body is taken as the essential characteristic of a Brāhmaṇa then, cremation of dead father would become *brahmahatyā* for his son. Therefore a Brāhmaṇa is (in the truest sense of the term) one, who on account of acquiring virtue, possesses purified inner-sense, becomes enriched with the four prerequisites (for the attainment of *Brahman*), posterior to the attainment of *saṁnyāsa* realizes, "It is *ātman*, the *Brahman*" by hearing, etc. (hearing reflecting, meditating) of the Vedānta texts. As is quoted in —

janmanā jāyate śūdro saṁskārāddvija ucyate ।
vedapāṭhādbhavedvipro brahma jānāti brāhmaṇaḥ ॥
— *Yatidharmasamuccaya*, 50

A śūdra takes emergence out of birth, he attains *dvija*hood after being initiated, becomes *vipra* by the study of Vedas and becomes brāhmaṇa only after attaining knowledge of *brahman*. **(10)**

By nature, the root principle is inanimate, that *mūla*, on account of its being enlightened by the Self-consciousness and possessing the superimposing relation, becomes the cause of this worldly appearance (*prapañca*); because the *smṛti* declares *mayādhyakṣeṇa prakṛtiḥ sūyate sacarācaram* (with me as the witnessing over the lord, the *prakṛti* gives birth to the world, with all its movable and immovable beings) (*Gīta*, 9/10); and the *śruti* says *devātmaśaktimiti* (the power belonging to God, himself) (*Śvet*., 1/3) This is the primal nescience or the witness of all this visible world by dint of Its inner power which is beginningless and imperishable, on account of its very subtle character (it) becomes the extreme cause just like a seed, the ignorance about this *mūla*, is primal nescience (*mūla-ājñānam*). **(11)** The nescience about a jar or about a cloth, on account of its being established by the direct perception and realized by the wise persons (who know perfectly) is therefore very unimportant, so it is called the subsidiary nescience (*tulā-ājñānam*). **(12)** As the crystal although known as transparent, still it appears red, because of its association with red flower, so also though the self is known as pure to the wise yet It seems to him, as the agent of this world, on account of its being connected with the internal organ, and It appears as the worldly appearance, due to the influence of his past deeds (*prārabdha karmas*) — it has been regarded as the attributive delusion (*sopādhika bhrama*). **(13)** That delusion, can be called as the attributeless, (*nirupādhika)*, where only on account of the erroneous perception, oystershell, pillar, etc., appear as the silver, human being, etc., so also to the ignorant person the worldly appearance appears to be the reality by imposing the agency of creation, etc., to the soul — this is (what is called) attributeless delusion. **(14)** Recognition (*pratyabhijñā*) — is that which is based on valid knowledge. For example — "This is that Devadatta," "I slept a sound sleep," "That thou art," "I am *Brahman*" (that, which is) — Thus recognized, is the recognition. **(15)**

The knowledge, which is produced only by past impression is called the recollection. It is of two types valid and invalid. Valid recollection is two-fold, recollection about non-self (*anātma-smṛti*) and that about the self (*ātma-smṛti*). Hence, this world is unreal because it is visible like the conch-shell-silver. To enquire of the falsity of this world is the valid non-self recollection. To search out the true import of the Upaniṣadic texts (like) "That thou art" — is the valid self-recollection. Invalid recollection also is of two types. Recollection of the self and that of the non-self. Just as before, the effort to prove the reality of this world is the invaild recollection on non-self. To see the self in egoism (*ahaṅkāra*) and the agency, etc., in the self is the invalid self-recollection — this is what is called — illusion (*bhrama*). **(16)** Impediments are of three types, past, present and future. From the study (of Vedānta) it appears, that the extreme attachment to any object before the *saṁnyāsa* is the past impediment. The attainment of another body on the removal of the past deeds (*prārabdha*s) as well as the attainment of *brahmaloka* — is the future impediment. The present one is fourfold: (1) attachment in favour of the objects in case of consideration, (2) the dullness of the intellect, (3) indulgence in bad reasonings, and (4) conviction of the self in the body. That is why it is uttered that, "Impediments of the present are known as (1) attachment to objects, (2) dullness of the intellect, (3) indulgence in bad logic, and (4) the unsurmountable false conviction (about the self) — these are the impediments." **(17)**

The removal of the past impediment is possible by the informative error (*saṁvādi bhrama*, i.e., by the meditation of attributeless *(nirguṇa) Brahman* and by chance realization of that. The future impediment is removed by birth alone. The removal of the present impediment occurs by hearing reflecting and meditating arising out of the renunciation. If the self-realization occurs to somebody with the help of analysis of the teachings of Vedānta, then it becomes a matter of examination, by which type of non-existence of the obstacles in respect to self-realization — the aforesaid impediments are dispelled. **(18)**

Apprehending the self as body, etc., means the continuation of beginningless nescience and this is what is called bondage. **(19)** The realization of the *brahman* in the self, takes place to one who possesses the prerequisites (for the attainment of self-knowledge) and acquires (the knowledge of) discrimination between the self and the non-self from the preceptor as well as from the scriptural texts. Because the *śruti* says: *brahmaiva san brahmāpyeti* (Being one with *Brahman*, he merges into *Brahman*) (*Bṛh*, 4/4/6, *NR̥ST*, 5). Therefore dispelling of nescience (*avidyā*) due to self-realization is known as Liberation. **(20)** The knowledge is two-fold, the empirical and the absolute. Of these (two), the empirical (one) owing to the difference of modification of the mind into active (*rājasa*) and passive (*tāmasa*) takes shape like knowledge of a jar, of a cloth, of the image of a deity, knowledge acquired by Yoga, knowledge of God, knowledge derived from the scriptural text, etc. (because) the modifications of the internal organ are innumerable. The absolute knowledge, however, is only one concerning self, which is purely illuminating — these are the varieties of knowledge. **(21)**

A jar is experienced by the knowledge of a jar, a cloth is experienced by the knowledge of a cloth, in this way realization takes places in respect of any thing up to the limit of God, etc., and of a particular deity, — such is the nature of those knowledge (as referred above). **(22)**

One and the same nescience is called *māyā* and *avidyā* due to difference of its projective and concealing power. Consciousness, associated with such type of nescience transforms itself into *jīva* (individual being) *īśvara* (the lord) and *jagat* (the cosmos). This is supported by the *śrutis* *ajāmekāṁ lohita-śukla-kṛṣnāṁ vahvīḥ prajāḥ sṛjamānāṁ sarūpām* (*Śvet.*, 4/5) (there is one unborn (feminine) being red, white and black producing numorous offspring of the same nature) *devātma śaktimiti* (the power belong-ing to illuminating self) (*Śvet.*, 1/

3), etc. For example, one king appears as if many, in a dream, this is what is known as the theory of single self (*ekajīvavāda*). Others, however acknowledge nescience as divided into collective and individual and manage to differentiate the theory of the individual soul (*jīva*) and the divine soul (*īśvara*). The followers of this section adhere to the theory of the plurality of soul (*anekajīvavāda*). Some, again are of opinion that consciousness, limited by the condition of the nescience, i.e. cause, is called divine soul or *īśvara* and that limited by the condition of the internal organ of productive nature i.e. effect is called the individual soul or *jīva*. In this school (we find) the emergence of the theory of appearance (*ābhāsavāda*) or the theory of reflection (*pratibimbavāda*). That is why it is said —

> *yayā yayā bhavet puṁsāṁ vyutpattiḥ pratyagātmani* ।
> *sā saiva prakriyā jñeyā sādhvī sā ca vyavasthiti* ॥
>
> — *Pañca.*, 8/73

> Whatever method helps one to understand clearly the indwelling *ātman* is the appropriate process and the correct measure.

That embodied soul may be termed as the *viśva*, *taijasa* and *prajñā* in accordance with variation of its states. All are unanimous on the point that *jīva* is so called because of its retention of vitality. This is what is known as *jīva*. **(23)**

The meaning of *jīva* is two-fold, viz., the primary meaning and the secondary meaning. That (consciousness) having the limitation due to association with five sheathes, is conveyed by the primary meaning (of the term *jīva*). All the three bodies come under these five sheaths, viz., the food sheath (*annamaya*) the vital (*prāṇamaya*), the mental (*manomaya*), the intellectual (*vijñānamya*), and the Bliss (*ānandamaya*) that (consciousness), not limited by those (five sheaths) is the secondary meaning (implied by *jīva*); these are however the two-fold meanings of *jīva*. **(24)**

That consciousness having *māyā*, as a limiting adjunct is the lord (*īśvara*). He is the lord: as it is approved in *śruti*, *māyāntu prakṛtiṁ vidyānmāyinantu maheśvaramiti* (know *māyā* as *prakṛti* and *Brahman* associated with *māyā*, as the great lord (*maheśvara*) (*Śvet.*, 4/10). **(25)** The term *īśvara* (lord) as referred above has two meanings (among them) one is primary and the other is secondary. The Consciousness bound with attributes known as the abode of creation, sustenance and dissolution and endowed with the qualities such as being the inner guide, omniscience, universal lordship, etc., is conveyed by the primary meaning (of the term *īśvara*). The reality of undivisible and unbound consciousness is the secondary meaning, implied by the term *īśvara* (the lord). **(26)**

Doubts are of three types (it is based on): (1) self, (2) god, and (3) their identification. As, whether it is a pillar or a human being or a monster so also whether the self is something other than the body, etc., or not, though (it is granted for that) it is separate, still whether it is an agent or non-agent, had it been taken for (that it is) a non-agent, still then whether it is consciousness as such or not, let it be accepted for consciousness as such, still whether it is bliss or not — such (a type of doubt) is about the self. Whether god is dual or not, had it been granted for secondless still, whether it is blissful or bliss as such (still), whether it is consciousness as such or not — it is about *paramātman* (the highest self). Though *jīva* is by nature existence consciousness and bliss as such (still) whether it is united with the Highest Self or not, though it is taken for united (still whether that realization becomes, the means of salvation or not, though it is (the means of salvation), whether that knowledge becomes the means of deliverance accompanied by the aid of *karman* or the consciousness alone — this is about the unification (between the individual self and the highest self). All these doubts are dispelled with the aid of study and reflecting on Vedānta. **(27)**

To take a thing for another (which is actually not that thing) is called the misapprehension. As to think a non-snake rope for a snake, likewise to apprehend the non-self for the self is the misapprehension. **(28)**

Brahman is the indivisible, non-dual, without any shape and therefore devoid of all types of difference, like the difference in species, etc. (difference of genus and that existing in oneself). That is supported by the Śruti: *ekamevād-vitīyam Brahman*, (*brahman* is one and without a second) (*Chān*., 6/2/1) *neha nānāsti kiñcana* (in it there is no diversity) (*Bṛh*., 4/4/19). It is *Brahman* because of its vastness. **(29)** *Saccidānanda svarūpam brahman* (*Brahman* is existence, consciousness and bliss as such), *satyaṁ jñānam anantaṁ brahmeti* (truth, knowledge and infinity is *Brahman*) (*Taitt*., 2/1/1, *Sarva*., 10) *ānando brahmeti* (*Brahman* is bliss) (*Taitt*., 3/6/1), in these texts Vedas declare the exact nature of *Brahman*. **(30)**

Following the path of a particular system and that is in the present case according to the *vṛtti* of Viśveśvara, the aspirant receives lessons in the prescribed way about *saṁnyāsa* from the *haṁsa* stage to *mānasa* stage, from the preceptor engrossed in *Brahman* — this is what is called *upasatti*. **(31)**

The interest, in respect of someone (who is) fortunate enough increases in the act of meditation on *Brahman*, this is what is known as *ekaparatva* (single-focus concentration). Just as a chaste woman likes to remain submerged in the thoughts of her husband. That is why it is said —

> *tat kathanaṁ taccintanamanyonyaṁ tat prabodhane* ।
> *etadaikyaparatvañca brahmābhyāsaṁvidur budhāḥ* ॥
> — *Pañca*., 7/106

> Thinking of him, speaking of him and making one another understand him — this is what the wise call single focus meditation or the concentration, same is called *Brahmābhyāsa*.

As said before (about the meditation on *Brahman*) the practice of hearing, reflecting and meditating on Vedānta constantly for a long time, till the realization of the identification of *jīva-Brahman* — is what is conveyed by the term *ekaparatva* (single-focus meditation). **(32)**

Anu means after, i.e., after the hearing, etc., by the process of *upasatti,* etc., and *bhava* means occurrence of self-realization in the form "I am *Brahman"* — this is what is meant by the term *anubhava,* i.e., the Transcendental Realization. **(33)** The division of implication is threefold, viz., *jahallakṣaṇā* (exclusive implication), *ajahallakṣanā* (inclusive implication) and *jahadajahallakṣaṇā* (exclusive-inclusive implication). For example, the cowherd lives on the Ganges, it is a case of exclusive implication, it is not applicable in the (analysis of the true import of) the sentence "Thou art that." Even non-exclusive implication like "The red (one) is running or (those on) the stage are making sounds" is not admissible in (ascertaining the true import of) "Thou art that" it follows therefore that *jahadajahallakṣaṇā* or exclusive-inclusive implication, i.e., the implication by which one part of the direct meaning of a sentence is given up and another part is retained applicable in the sentence like "This is that Devadatta" is possible in the case of (ascertaining the import of) the great sentence *tattvamasi,* i.e., "That thou art." In the import of the word *tat* the part meaning Undivisible consciousness is retained by abandoning the part i.e. expressing indirectness. In the context of Thou, i.e., *tvam* what remains as residual meaning is the Absolute Pure consciousness leaving out the part i.e. meaning expressive of directness. And that "I am *Brahman"* comes out as a resultant full meaning of the sentence *tattvamasi* becomes a ground of implicative efficiency of exclusive-inclusive type. **(34)**

Just as milk itself is turned into curd, so also *prakṛti* or *māyā* itself which is denoted by the word *pradhāna,* is transformed into the shape of this world. Similarly *mahat* sprang out form *māyā, ahaṅkāra* (egoism) came out from *mahat* and from the *ahaṅkāra* came out the five subtle elements and therefrom sprang forth five gross bodies. Such a law is, what is known as the theory of evolution (*pariṇāmavāda*). **(35)**

Just as a large number of grains of soil being assembled make a jar in turn, as a large number of fibres (by the process of weaving and knitting) make a cloth, so also numrous atoms being accumulated in turn, build up this world — this is (called) the theory of origination according to the Naiyāyikas. **(36)**

The causal factors are of three types, viz., the *pariṇāma* (transformation), *ārambha* (origination) and the *vivarta* (phenomenon). In the theory of evolution, the spontaneous transformation of *māyā*, is not possible, because in that case there, would be contradiction with *śruti, devātma śaktimiti* (the power belonging to god himself) (*Śvet.*, 1/3), etc., and because of the fact that the absolute primordial substance is inanimate by nature. Even in the theory of origination atoms are said to be partless and therefore the connection of atoms become impossible and diversity (of creation) cannot be accounted for. What remains therefore to be possible, is the causal factor of illusory appearance, as it is supported by the *śruti* — *parāsya śaktir vividhaiva śrūyate svābhāvikī jñāna vala kriyāca* (his high power is revealed to be various, indeed. The working of his intelligence and strength is inherent (in him)) (*Śvet.*, 6/8).

It is *Brahman* itself which (by dint of its own power) becomes the material cause as well as the efficient cause by its conscient portion. And in this way, monism is established on account of the falsity of the inconceivable nescience, etc. This is (what is called) *vivartavāda* (theory of illusory appearance). **(37)**

According to the Naiyāyikas there are four sources of valid knowledge, perception, inference, analogy and verbal testimony. According to Vedāntins the *pramāṇa*s (sources of valid knowledge) are six in number, viz., perception, inference, analogy, verbal testimony, postulation and non-cognition. According to Purāṇas, these aforesaid six along with tradition (*aitihya*) and inclusion (*sambhava*) make the *pramāṇa*s eight in number. The verbal testimony is the strongest among all these *pramāṇa*s. The Vedic dictums, viz., *tattvamasi* (That Thou art), *ahaṁ brahmāsmi* (I am *Brahman*) — are the proofs. **(38)**

The disciple possessing the four *sādhana*s, i.e., the

prerequisites for the study of Vedānta follows his preceptor. That is why it is quoted —

> *praśāntacittāya jitendriyāya prahīṇadoṣāya yathoktakāriṇe* ।
> *guṇānvitāyānugatāya sarvadā pradeyametat satataṁ mumukṣave* ॥
> — *Upa. Sā.*, 16/72

This is always to be taught to one, who is of tranquil mind, who has subjugated his senses, who is free from faults, obedient, endowed with virtues, always submissive and who is constantly eager for liberation.

The disciple (*śiṣya*) means one who is eligible for the study of Vedānta and that is already determined in the context, of narrating the preliminaries. This is what is meant by the term *śiṣya*. **(39)** The *guru* or preceptor is one, who knows the true import of the Vedas, remains steadfast in *Brahman*, trustworthy and whose capability of convincing others is added with a mark of glory. The meaning of the term *guru* follows from the *śruti* as *samitpāṇiḥ śrotriyaṁ brahmaniṣṭhaṁ gurum upagacchet* (with fuel in hand one should go to a preceptor who is learned in the Vedas and absorbed in *Brahman*) (*Muṇḍ.*, 1/2/12). **(40)**

Just as, the removing of coldness is the specific characteristics of fire, or healing of the acute disease is the specific characteristic of the mineral medicine — so the defining characteristic of a preceptor is to impart peace to his own disciple, who takes refuge in him and who is suffering from three types of pains (*ādhibhautika,* i.e., inanimate objects, *ādhidaivika,* i.e., supernatural and *ādhyāmika,* i.e., internal) of this world from the time immemorial. That is why, it is quoted, —

> *'gu' śabdasyāndhakārasya 'ru' śabdastannirodhakaḥ* ।
> *andhakāraniruddhatvādgururityabhidhīyate* ॥
> — *Gurugītā,* 19

As the syllable *gu* means darkness and *ru* means that

which dispells it, so one is called *guru*, on account of his power of dispelling darkness.

This is the defining characteristics of *guru*. **(41)**

It is *ātman*, as it walks on constantly; or what is knowable is the self and self only. *Ātman* is immutable, non-agent, the *sākṣin* (witness) of inanimate objects like the body, *ahaṅkāra* (egoism), etc. It is supported by the *śruti* — *asaṅgohyayaṁ puruṣo* (this *puruṣa* is independent) (*Bṛh.*, 4/3/15), there is another famous *śruti*, *ayamātmā sarvāntaraḥ* (*Bṛh.*, 3/5/1). (this soul is immanent). This soul can be immanent on account of its being witness of everybody/everything just as a king in his own court. Even the wise (men) feel "I am independent, I am immutable (without any change) — this is what is meant by the term *ātmā*." **(42)**

He is *paramātman* (the highest soul), highest in the sense that he is the excellent soul among the body, etc. The appearance of the reflection of consciousness (itself) in the *jīva*'s intellect — is the secondary meaning *eṣa indra eṣa varuṇa eṣa sarveśvaraḥ* (this is Indra, this is Varuṇa, this is Sarveśvaraḥ; the universal lord) (*Māṇḍ.*, 4/4/6) *tasya bhāsā sarvamidaṁ bibhāti* (It is due to his enlightening power, everything becomes illuminated) (*Muṇḍ.*, 2/2/10; *Kaṭha.*, 2/2/15; *Śvet.*, 6/14) what appears from these Vedic sentences is the true import of the term *paramātman*. **(43)**

The renunciation is of four types. One, who is endowed with the acute non-attachment belongs to *kuṭīcara* or *bahūdaka* type of *saṁnyāsa*. The person, who being aware of the difference between the self and the non-self, is endowed with more acute non-attachment, is adhering to the *haṁsa* type of *saṁnyāsa*. After self-realization rejection of the tuft of hair, sacrificial thread, etc., by a person who is already attached to extreme non-attachment — this is what is known as *paramahaṁsa* (type of *saṁnyāsa*) in the scriptures, this very type again is called the *saṁnyāsa* of scholarly order (*vidvat saṁnyāsa*). These are the respective meanings of *saṁnyāsa*. As the lord advocates —

> *sarva karmāṇi manasā saṁnyasyāste sukhaṁ vaśī* ।
> *navadvāre pure dehī naiva kurvannakārayanniti* ॥
> — *Gītā*, 5/13

> The embodied man of self control, making over all the works mentally continues happily in the city of mine gateways, neither doing anything, nor causing (the body) to do any work.

As the *śruti* reads — *brahma-caryādeva vrajet, gṛhasthādeva pravrajet vānaprasthādevetyādi* (one should resign from the order of celebacy (*brahmacarya*), as well as from the domestic order (*gārhasthya*) and from the order of secluded life (*vānaprastha*), etc. (*Jābāl.*, 4). Therefore the rejection of works totally is the renunciation (*saṁnyāsa*), and this is conveyed by the word *sannyāsa*. **(44)**

The division of relinquishment (*tyāga*) is of two types; viz., that of the results of deeds (*karma-phala-tyāga*) and that of the visible world (*dṛśya-tyāga*). Of them the relinquishment of the results of deeds, is advocated in the text of *Gītā* by the Almighty God —

> *anāśritaḥ karmaphalaṁ kāryaṁ karma karoti yaḥ* ।
> *sa saṁnyāsī ca yogī ca na niragnir nacākriyaḥ* ॥
> — *Gītā*, 6/1

> He, who having not expected the results of deeds, renders duties (regarding such performance) as an end itself is a monk and a *yogī* but not so is the one, who does not keep sacrificial fire nor one who does not perform the prescribed duties.

Here the rejection of *karman* has been praised as the essence of renunciation and preached to a commoner, who is not attached to the path of knowledge. The giving up of the visible world has been instructed by my preceptor Śri Mādhavānanda Muni is as follows: Pay heed to him, I am *Brahman*, devoid of three *guṇa*s, free from five *pāśa*s (fetters) destitute of six *bhāva*s (modes) as well as six *ūrmi*s (modifications) and pure (without any blemish). The status of Brahmā, Viṣṇu and Maheśvara is beyond the limitation of worldly appearance. In this world *jīvas* are of various characters but I don't know where all these (modes and modifications) have been dispelled, at the dawn of my absolute (pure) knowledge just like a dream. Removal of the nescience along with that of the deeds belongs to the knowers of oneness of *Brahman* and *ātman*. This is what is meant by *tyāga* or relinquishment. **(45)**

Sva means exact nature of the self and this exact nature of self is implied by the word *ātman*, in which the body, the sense-organs, the vital force and the internal organ also, on account of their being superimposed, are regarded as *ātman*. This *ātman* is known as *pratyagātman* (indwelling self) *eṣa sa ātmā sarvasyāntaraḥ* (this is that *ātman*, who is emanent everywhere) (*Bṛh.*, 3/5/1). By the force of this Vedic text, the connotation of the word *svarūpa* should be taken as above. **(46)**

This *ātman* is non-agent. That is why, it is quoted —

yasya nā haṅ kṛtobhāvo buddhir yasya na lipyate ।
hatvāpi sa imāṁllokānna hantina nibadhyate ॥
— *Gītā*, 18/17

He, who has no feeling of egoism and whose intellect is not tainted (by any attachment) he doesn't kill nor does he become bound (by the consequences of the action) even by killing all the creatures.

prakṛtyaiva ca karmāṇi kriyamāṇāni sarvaśaḥ ।
yaḥ paśyati tathātmānamakartāraṁ sa paśyati ॥
— *Gītā*, 13/29

He, who sees actions, as being done universally by the nature alone and the self similarly, as not the agent — he sees (the self as it is).

Asaṅgohyayam puruṣa (this *puruṣa* is independant) (*Bṛh.*, 4/3/5) this Vedic dictum makes it clear that this is implied by the term "non-agent." **(47)**

It is the *ātman*, which cannot be refuted by any object in all the three ages — it is also termed as the witness. It is supported by (the lines from *Pañcadaśī*, 3/29),

> *satyatvaṁ bādharāhityaṁ jagadvādhaikasākṣiṇaḥ* ।
> *bādhaḥ kiṁ sākṣī ko brūhi natvasākṣī ka iṣyate* ॥

> Existence is that which, cannot be negated. If the Self, which is the witness of this perishable world, becomes perishable then who will be the witness to the fact of its perishability? For destruction without a witness can not be postulated.

Satyaṁ jñānamanantaṁ brahma (*Brahman* is truth, knowledge and unlimited) (*Taitt.*, 2/1/1, Sarva. 10), *yat satyaṁ sa ātmā* (it is the *ātman*, which is Truth itself) (*Chān.*, 6/8/3, 6/4/4), *sadeva saumya idamagra āsīdekamevādvitīyam brahma* (O my son! there was only one existence, in the past, i.e., *Brahman* the one and without a second) (*Chān.*, 6/2/1); these Vedic texts (justify that) he is eternal as well as the only truth. He is implied by the term *vastu*. **(48)** *Cit* means self-luminous, which is known to be the witness of the fourth state of the consciousness by the application of the method of agreement and difference (*anvaya-vyatireka*), the automatically established non-divisible pure consciousness. *Ayaṁ puruṣo svayaṁjyotir bhavati* (this being becomes self-luminous) (*Bṛh.*, 4/3/9), *tasya bhāsā sarvam idaṁ bibhāti* (It is his lustre, which illumines all these things) (*Muṇḍ.*, 2/2/10; *Kaṭha.*, 2/1/15; *Śvet.*, 6/14). This is the true import of the term *cit* known from the Vedic texts. **(49)**

Bliss is the abode of the great love itself. That is why it is said (in *Pañcadaśī*, 12/72).

> *parapremās-padatvena paramānandarūpatā* ।
> *sukhavṛddhiḥ prītivṛddhau sārvabhaumādiṣu śrutā* ॥

> The very nature of the supreme bliss is due to its being the abode of supreme love. The *śruti* (*Taitt.*, 2/8/1-2/8/5; *Bṛh.*, 4/3/33) declares that from the sovereignty of this world up to the position of *hiraṇyagarbha*

wherever there is greater love there is greater bliss.

In the *Bṛhadāraṇyakopaniṣat* Yājñavalkya made instructions to Maitrayī,

> *na vā are putrakāmāya putraḥ priyo bhavati ātmanastu kāmāya putraḥ priyo bhavati . . . na vā are sarvaṁ kāmāya sarvaṁ priyaṁ bhavati ātmanastu kāmāya sarvaṁ priyaṁ bhavati*
> — *Bṛh.*, 4/5/6

The speech starts with "It is not that a son becomes dear to his father for the sake of son but for his own sake" and ends with the following, "it is not that all are lovable for their sake, but it is for the sake of one's own." Moreover

> *. . . ānando brahma . . . ānandāddhyeva khalvimāni bhūtāni jāyante, ānandena jātāni jīvanti tat prayantyabhi saṁviśanti*
> — *Taitt.*, 3/6

> *. . . brahma-puccha pratiṣṭhā*
> — *Taitt.*, 2/5

Brahman is bliss as such. All the creatures are brought forth from the bliss, these being are sustained by the bliss and finally they are reabsorbed therein. *Brahman* is the lower part, the foundation. From these Vedic dictums and logical statements, it is established that *Brahman* is Bliss as such. Even from the realization of the wise that "I am Existence Consciousnes-bliss as such", This meaning of the word *ānanda* becomes evident. **(50)**

Infinity means the property of being unlimited by space, time and matter or the property of being free from the difference present among the objects belonging to the same class (*sajātīyabheda*), that, present among objects belonging to the divergent classes (*vijātīya bheda*) and that difference which belongs to a whole entity and its component parts (*svagata bheda*). It is bereft of the limitation of space as it pervades all. As it is eternal, it cannot be limited by time. As it is immanent in everything, it cannot be taken as limited by any particular object. Consciousness, different from the inanimate groups is but one only. Therefore no question arises in respect of god and the individual self as to the presence of difference belonging to the same class. Due to its manifestation in varieties the universe cannot be regarded as reality (*vastu*) and therefore such type of difference belonging to the objects of divergent groups cannot be taken as present in the case of conscious element and the universe. And the difference among the whole and its parts also does not hold good here because of the very nature of oneness of *Brahman* and *ātman* and its character of being devoid of any component element. It is supported by the *smṛti*-text (*Gītā,* 10/42) *viṣṭabhyāhamidaṁ kṛtsnamekāṁśena sthitojagat* (I stand controlling and regulating all this universe with but a fraction of my power) and again the *śruti* says *pādoasya viśvā bhūtāni tripādasti svayaṁ-prabhaḥ* (Creation is only a quarter of *brahman* the other three quarters are self-revealing) (*Chān.,* 3/12/6; *PS,* 3). *Śatyaṁ jñānamanantaṁ brahma* (*Brahman* is existence consciousness and eternal, etc.) (*Taitt.,* 2/1/1, *Sarva.,* 10). Therefore that infinite self is referred to by the term *ananta*. **(51)**

The unification of *jīva* (self) and *īśvara* (self) by applying *jahadajahallakṣaṇā,* is implied by the term *ekatā,* i.e., identification. For example, in the sentence "This is that Devadatta" the word that signifying Devadatta characterized by the former time and the word "this" signifying Devadatta characterized by the present time, Devadatta only is meant by negating the attributes like this and that. Similarly in case of "That Thou Art" the word "that" signifying consciousness characterized by remoteness and the word "thou" signifying consciousness characterized by immediacy, all the contrary ideas are negated and the one and the same immutable consciousness is taken into account. In that case, the difference between *jīva* and *īśvara* is accidental and not a real one. This is supported (by the verse of *Pañcadaśī,* 6/237).

> *kūṭastha brahmaṇorbhedo nāmamātrād ṛte na hi* ।
> *ghaṭākāśa mahākāśau vijujyete na hi kvacit* ॥

> The difference between *kūṭastha* and *Brahman*, is only by name, in reality there is no difference because the sky limited by a pot and the unlimited sky (i.e., *mahākāśa*) are not distinct from one another.

Its true import is explained hereby: as one and the same sky becomes of four types, viz., (1) the *megha-ākāśa* (the sky associated with cloud) (2) *ghaṭa-ākāśa* (the sky limited by jar), (3) *jala-ākāśa* (the sky conditioned by water) and (4) *mahā-ākāśa* (all-embracing sky). The sky reflected in the water of jar, is the sky conditioned by the water (i.e., *jala-ākāśa*). The *ghaṭa-ākāśa* and *mahākāśa* (all-embracing sky) appear to be the same to the intelligent one (who has sense of differentiation) even though the sky conditioned by the water and the cloud are ignored. So also it is one and the same consciousness becomes (1) *īśvara* associated with *māyā* (2) the *kūṭastha*, (3) the *cidābhāsa jīva* (the consciousness reflected in ignorance) and (4) *akhaṇḍa saccidānanda* (Indivisible Being, Consciousness-cum-Bliss). However, if the *īśvara* and *jīva* are left, the self-reliant can realize the identification of *kūṭastha brahma*. I am, I feel, I shall ever be dear, this is the implied meaning of *jīva* as well as of *īśvara*. That Being Consciousness Bliss is to be realized as I am *brahma*. With the dawn of this knowledge, the mortal becomes immortal one.

As the eye perceives, its own formation, reflected in the mirror, similarly it is the soul which visualize its own Being Consciousness-cum-Bliss nature reflected in the pure intellect. Soul is subjected to the modification of *ahaṁ*, this is the Visualization as well as Transcendental Realization. The person having such a realization is blessed indeed. All his accumulated deeds are destroyed and he is not tainted by future deeds. Self-reliant, is not the agent. With the dawn of pure knowledge (*brahma-jñāna*), the primal nescience is dispelled and all his lusts are scorched up by the light of Self-Knowledge. He observes all the functions, performed in the body, sense-organs and mind, as a result of past deeds and lives like *jīvanmukta* (emancipated while alive). With the accomplishment of enjoying past deeds, he becomes Indivisible Being Consciousness Bliss as such. This is approved by the saying *yā matiḥ sā gatir bhavet* (the ultimate attainment of the individual should be according to his own intention). Regarding this unification the saying of *śruti, smṛti, itihāsas* and Purāṇas are proofs. Because it is cited (in *Śvet. Up.*, 6/11) —

> *eko devaḥ sarva bhūteṣu gūḍhaḥ*
> *sarvavyāpī sarva bhūtāntarātmā* ।
>
> *karmādhyakṣaḥ sarvabhūtādhivāsaḥ*
> *sākṣicetā kevalo nirguṇaśca* ॥

> The, one god hidden in all beings, all-pervading the inner self of all beings, the ordainer of all deeds who dwells in all beings, the witness, the knower, the only one, devoid of qualities.

Moreover it is supported by the *śruti* texts *ekamevādvitiyaṁ brahma* (*brahma* is one and without a second) (*Chān.*, 6/2/1), *neha nānāsti kiñcana* (in it there is no diversity) (*Bṛh.*, 4/4/19), *tattvamasi* (That Thou Art) (*Chān.*, 6/8/7, 6/9/4, 6/10/3, 6/11/3, 6/12/3, 6/13/3, 6/14/3, 6/15/3, 6/16/3) *ahaṁ brahmāsmi* (I am *brahman*) (*Bṛh.*, 1/4/10), *jñātvā devaṁ mucyate sava-pāśaiḥ* (by knowing god the soul is freed from all fetters), (*Śvet. Up.*, 1/8, 2/15, 4/26, 5/13, 6/13) *tasya tāvadeva ciraṁ yāvanna vimokṣye* (I shall remain here only, so long as I shall not be released (from ignorance) (*Chān.*, 6/14/2), *vimuktaśca vimucyate* (freed soul is being freed indeed) (*Kaṭha*. 4/2). (It is supported by the verses of *Gītā* also.)

> *kṣetrajñañcāpi māṁ viddhi sarva-kṣetreṣu bhārata* ।
> *kṣetra-kṣetrajñayorjñānaṁ yattaj jñānaṁmataṁ mama* ॥
> — 13/2
>
> *yathā sarvagataṁ saukṣmyādākāśaṁ nopalipyate* ।
> *sarvatrāvasthitodehe tathātmā nopalipyate* ॥
> — 13/32
>
> *yathā prakāśayatyekaḥ kṛtsnaṁ lokamimaṁ raviḥ* ।
> *kṣetraṁ kṣetrī tathākṛtsnaṁ prakāśayati bhārata* ॥
> — 13/33

O descendent of Bharata dynasty: know me to be the knower of the field (*kṣetrajña*) in all the fields. In my view, the highest knowledge is that which is (knowledge) of the body and also of the knower of the body.

As all-pervading ether is not tainted by reason of its subtlety, so also the self, though stationed in the body everywhere is not tainted.

As a single sun illumines up this whole world, even so, O Bharata: the lord of the body illumines the whole field.

> *ātmānaṁ vindate yastu sarvabhūtaguhāśayam* ।
> *ślokena yadi vārdhena kṣīṇaṁ tasya prayojanam* ॥

The person, who attains the self, hidden in the heart of all the beings has hardly any necessity for a verse or hemistich.

> *jyotirūpam arūpañca svarūpaṁ hṛdi saṁsthitam* ।
> *sarvajñaṁ sarva-bhūtasthaṁ sarveśam sarvato mukham* ॥

The exact nature of the self is luminous and at the same time it is without any form. (It is) residing in the core of heart, omniscient pervaded in all the beings, the lord of everyone and facing in all the directions.

It is the *Brahman*, the indivisible self, the Being Consciousness-Bliss as such, is the non-dual Self. This is implied by the term *ekatā*, i.e., the identification of Supreme Self and the individual self. **(52)**

Knowing this Self, you may attain success (i.e., the *summum-bonum*).

4

Similar References

1. अनुबन्धः —
   *के अनुबन्धाः ?
   प्रश्नावली ॥१॥ (क) वेदान्तसारः ५-२९
   (ख) सर्ववेदान्तसिद्धान्तसारसंग्रहः ।६-१६ ।

2. प्रकृतिः —
   का प्रकृतिः ?
   प्रश्नावली ॥२॥ पंचदशी १/१५
   "अनादि सान्ता गुणानां साम्यावस्था प्रकृतिः ।" cf. "चिदानन्दमयब्रह्म प्रतिविम्बसमन्विता । तमरजःसत्त्वगुणा प्रकृतिर्द्विविधा च सा ॥"

3. माया —
   *का माया ?
   प्रश्नावली ॥३॥ (क) पंचदशी १/१५-१६
   "शुद्धसत्त्वप्रधाना सा ईश्वरोपाधिर्माया ।" cf. ". . . . प्रकृतिर्द्विविधा च सा ॥ सत्त्वशुद्धयविशुद्धिभ्यां मायाऽविद्ये च ते मते ।"

---

1. *There is strong affinity of the present text with that of *Vedāntasāra* and *Sarvavedānta-Siddhāntasārasaṁgraha,* with only difference in the style of presentation. The fore-cited works discussed the topic in an illustrative way whereas Jaḍa-Bharata has done the same in a nutshell form.

3. *On this point Jaḍa-Bharata has been influenced by *Sarvavedānta-siddhāntasāra-saṁgraha* and *Pañcadaśī,* though *Vidyāraṇya*'s theory of *māyā* is more lucid as well as illustrative. Here Jaḍa-Bharata has given only a definition of the term.

(ख) सिद्धान्तलेशसंग्रहः पृ० ११०
cf. "त्रिगुणात्मिकायाः मूलप्रकृतेः . . . "माया चाविद्या च स्वयमेव भवती"ति श्रुतिसिद्धौ द्वौ रूपभेदौ। रजस्तमोनभिभूत शुद्धसत्त्व- प्रधाना माया; . . . एकैव मूल प्रकृते-र्विक्षेपप्राधान्येन मायाशब्दिते-श्वरोपाधिः।"

(ग) वेदान्तसारः ॥३७॥
cf. " . . . उत्कृष्टोपाधितया शुद्धसत्त्वप्रधाना॥"

(घ) सर्ववेदान्तसिद्धान्तसारसंग्रहः ॥३११॥
cf. "इयं समष्टिरुत्कृष्टं सत्त्वाशोतुत्कर्षतः पुरा। मायेति कथ्यते तज्ज्ञैः शुद्धसत्त्वैक-लक्षणा॥"

(ङ) वाक्यसुधा ॥३५॥

(च) प्रकटार्थविवरणम् — १म अः पृ० ३।

4. अविद्या —

*का अविद्या ?
प्रश्नावली ॥४॥
"मायायाः कतिपयांशै-र्मलिनसत्त्वप्रधाना जीवोपाधिरविद्या।

(क) पंचदशी १/१५-१६
cf. " . . . प्रकृतिर्द्विविधा च सा॥ सत्त्वशुद्ध्यविशुद्धिभ्यां मायाऽविद्ये च ते मते।"

---

4. *Avidyā, being a vital point of Advaita Vedānta has been handled by so many authors, variously. Here the present text has defined only the term and in that case it shows striking similarity with that of *Pañcadaśī* and *Siddhāntaleśasaṁgraha*. Other works have dealt with the topic more vividly and given more clear views. They have discussed the subject and locus of *avidyā*, its functions, varieties and characteristic features.

According to Śaṅkara, Padmapāda and Prakāśātman *avidyā* and *māyā* are all the same, their difference is very indistinct. Jaḍa-Bharata holds the same view.

"माया चाविद्या स्वय-
मेव भवतीति श्रुतेः।"

(ख) सिद्धान्तलेशसंग्रहः पृ० ११०
cf. "त्रिगुणात्मिकायाः मूलप्रकृतेः . . . "माया चाविद्या च स्वयमेव भवती"ति श्रुतिसिद्धौ द्वौ रूपभेदौ। रजस्तमोनभिभूत शुद्धसत्त्वप्रधाना माया स्तदभिभूतमलिन-सत्त्वा त्वविद्येति। . . ."

(ग) वेदान्तसारः ॥४२॥
cf. "इयंव्यष्टिः निकृष्टोपाधितया मलिनसत्त्व प्रधाना।"

(घ) प्रकटार्थ-विवरणम् — १म अः पृ० ३

(ङ) सर्ववेदान्त-सिद्धान्तसारसंग्रहः ॥३४॥

(च) आत्मबोधः पृ० ४५०

(छ) इष्टसिद्धिः १/१४०

(ज) अद्वैतसिद्धिः पृ० ५४६

(झ) नैष्कर्म्यसिद्धिः ३/६६

(ञ) आत्मानात्मविवेकः पृ० ५

(ट) ब्रह्मसिद्धिः पृ० ९

(ठ) निर्वाणदशकम् पृ० ७१

(ड) प्रत्यक्तत्त्वप्रदीपिका ॥३९॥

(ढ) संक्षेपशारीरकम् १/३१९, २/२०

5. अपंचीकृत पंचमहाभूतानि —

1. कान्यपंचीकृतपंचभूतानि ?

प्रश्नावली ॥५॥ — (क) वेदान्तसारः ॥५५॥

*2. कथमेतेषामुत्पत्तिः

प्रश्नावली ॥६॥
"तस्मादात्मन आकाशः सम्भूतः आकाशाद्वायुः वायोरग्निरग्नेरापोरद्भ्यः

(क) तैत्तिरीयोपनिषत् २/१/३
cf. "तस्माद्वा एतस्मादात्मन आकाशः सम्भूतः आकाशाद्वायुः वायोरग्निः अग्नेरापः। अद्भ्यः पृथिवी . . .।"

---

*On this point, Jaḍa-Bharata himself doesn't show any originality but referred to *Taitt. Up.* only.

पृथिवी" चेत्यापि श्रुतेरेवं
तेषामुत्पत्तिः।"

(ख) मुण्डकोपनिषत् १/१/८, २/१/३
(ग) पंचदशी १/१८
(घ) पंचीकरणम् - ॥१॥
(ङ) सर्ववेदान्तसिद्धान्तसारसंग्रहः ॥३३६-३३८॥

**3. कानि नामकानि च ?
प्रश्नावली ॥६॥

(क) पंचदशी १/१८, ४/४
(ख) पंचीकरणम् ॥१॥

6. सूक्ष्मशरीरम् —
किं सूक्ष्मशरीरम्
प्रश्नावली - ॥७॥

(क) सर्ववेदान्तसिद्धान्तसारसंग्रहः ॥३४०-३४१॥
(ख) आत्मबोधः ॥१२॥
(ग) पंचीकरणवार्त्तिकम् ॥३१-३६॥
(घ) आत्मानात्मविवेकः पृ० १९
(ङ) पंचदशी १/२३
(च) संक्षेपशारीरकम् ३/१९
(छ) वेदान्तसारः ५८, ६७-६८, ७३-७६

7. पंचीकृतपंचमहाभूतानि —
1. कानि पंचीकृतपंचभूतानि ?
प्रश्नावली ॥८॥

(क) पंचीकरणम् - ॥ १॥
(ख) पंचीकरणविवरणम् - पृ० ५८
(ग) पंचदशी १/२६-२७
(घ) सर्ववेदान्तसिद्धान्तसारसंग्रहः ॥३८८- ४०३॥

** Although the third part of the Q.No. 6 demands the names of non-quintuplicated rudimentary elements, Jaḍa-Bharata kept silence, whereas *Pañcadaśī*, *Pañcīkaraṇam*, etc., gave the names separately.

2. कथमेतेषामुत्पत्तिः ?

प्रश्नावली ॥९॥ (क) वेदान्तसारः ८७-५५, ९२
(ख) सर्ववेदान्तसिद्धान्तसारसंग्रहः ॥४३२-४३५॥

8. ब्राह्मणः —
*को ब्राह्मणो जीवो वा जाति र्वा पाण्डित्यं वा कर्म वा देहो वा ?

प्रश्नावली ॥१०॥ (क) वज्रसूचिकोपनिषत् - १क-१ज पृ० ३८७-३८९
(ख) वज्रसूची - क-ध, पृ० २-५
(ग) अस्सलायनसुत्त - मज्झिमनिकाय ४४ अ. पृ० ४०५-४१०

9. मूलाऽज्ञानम् —
* किं मूलाऽज्ञानम् ?

प्रश्नावली - ॥११॥ (क) पंचदशी - ६/२५
(ख) "सर्ववेदान्तसिद्धान्तसारसंग्रहः" ॥४८९-४९०॥
(ग) विरचितार्थबोधिनीटीका on वेदान्त-परिभाषा, प्रत्यक्षःपरिः - पृ० ५७

*10. तुलाऽज्ञानम् —

---

8. *It was a practice among the different scholars of different branches of learning to raise points on the nature of *brāhmaṇa* and Jaḍa-Bharata also, is not an exception to this point. His definition of *brāhmaṇa* may not be beyond criticism. But his definition is free from ambiguity and incompleteness.

9. *Jaḍa-Bharata tries to define the term *mūlājñānam* with the support of quotations from the *Gītā*, 9/10 and the *Śvet. Up.*, 1/3, still the idea has become somewhat cumbrūss, on account of the incorrect reading of the text.

   The fore-cited works, specially the *Viracitārthabodhinī* gloss on *Vedāntaparibhāṣā* has given a clear view on this point.

10. *According to the above-mentioned treatise *mūlājñānam* and *tūlājñānam* are the same. Their difference is negligible but Jaḍa-Bharata has shown the division distinctly.

किं तुलाऽज्ञानम् ?

प्रश्नावली ॥१२॥ (क) वेदान्तसंज्ञावली - ॥४२॥
(ख) विरचितार्थबोधिनीटीका on वेदान्त-परिभाषा, प्रत्यक्षःपरिः - पृ० ५७

11. सोपाधिकः भ्रमः —
कः सोपाधिको भ्रमः ?

प्रश्नावली ॥१३॥ (क) तत्त्वानुसन्धानम् - ३य परिः पृ० ३४
(ख) सर्ववेदान्तसिद्धान्तसारसंग्रहः - ४८०-४८१

12. निरुपाधिकः भ्रमः —
कः निरुपाधिको भ्रमः ?

प्रश्नावली ॥१४॥ (क) तत्त्वानुसन्धानम् - ३य परिः पृ० ३४
(ख) सर्ववेदान्तसिद्धान्तसारसंग्रहः - ४८०-४८१

13. प्रत्यभिज्ञा —
का प्रत्यभिज्ञा ?

प्रश्नावली ॥१५॥ (क) पंचपादिका - पृ० ८-१०
(ख) पंचपादिकाविवरणम् - पृ० ७५
(ग) विवरणप्रमेयसंग्रहः - पृ० १३६

14. भ्रमः -
कः भ्रमः ?

प्रश्नावली ॥१६॥ (क) तत्त्वानुसन्धानम्-३य परिः पृ० ३२

"संस्कारमात्रजन्य ज्ञानं स्मृतिः। साऽपि द्विविधा। यथार्थाऽयथार्थाचेति।यथार्था स्मृति द्विविधा, अनात्म स्मृतिरात्मस्मृतिश्च। तत्रायं प्रपंचो मिथ्या, दृश्यत्वात्-शुक्तिरूप्यवत्। एतस्य मिथ्यात्वाऽनुसन्धानं यथार्थाऽनात्मस्मृतिः। तत्त्वमस्यादिवाक्यार्थाऽनुसंधानं यथार्थाऽत्मस्मृतिश्च।अयथार्था-

cf. "संस्कार मात्रजन्यं ज्ञानं स्मृतिः। साऽपिद्विविधा। यथार्थाऽयथार्थभेदात्। यथार्थस्मृतिरपि द्विविधा, अनात्मस्मृतिरात्मस्मृतिश्चेति। तत्रं व्यवहारिकप्रपंचोमिथ्या दृश्यत्वात् . . . शुक्तिरूप्यवदित्यनुमानसिद्धमिथ्यात्वाऽनुसंधानं यथार्थाऽनात्मस्मरणम्। तत्त्वमस्यादिवाक्यार्थाऽनुसंधानं यथार्थाऽत्मस्मरणम्। अयथार्था स्मृतिरपि द्विविधा अनात्मस्मृतिरात्मस्मृतिश्च। पूर्ववत् प्रपंचस्य सत्यत्वाऽनुसंधानमयथार्थाऽनात्मस्मरणम्।. . . अहङ्कारा-

स्मृतिरपिद्विविधा अनात्म-
स्मृतिरात्मस्मृतिश्च ।पूर्ववत्
प्रपंचस्य सत्यत्वाऽनुसंधानम-
यथार्थानात्मस्मृतिः। अहङ्कारा-
दिष्वात्मत्वामुसन्धानम-
यथार्थाऽत्मस्मृतिरयं भ्रमः।"

दिष्वात्मत्वानुसन्धानमात्मनि कर्त्तृत्वाद्यनु-
सन्धानं यथार्थाऽऽत्मस्मरणम्। अयं
भ्रमः।"
(ख) स्वात्मनिरूपणम् ॥८६॥
(ग) उपदेशसाहस्री १६/१९।

15. प्रतिबन्धाः

1. के प्रतिबन्धाः ?

प्रश्नावली - ॥१७॥

(क) पंचदशी - ९/३९। ४३
(ख) तत्त्वानुसन्धानम् - ३य परिः पृ० ३५।

*2. तेषां निवृत्तिः कथम् ?

प्रश्नावली - ॥१८॥

(क) पंचदशी - ९/४१-४५
(ख) तत्त्वानुसंधानम् - ३य परिः, पृ० ३५

16. बन्धः -

कः बन्धः ?

प्रश्नावली - ॥१९॥

(क) पंचदशी - ७/३७ - १०/४
(ख) उपदेशसाहस्री - १६/५८
(ग) विवरणप्रमेयसंग्रहः पृ० ४९

17. मोक्षः -

कः मोक्षः ?

प्रश्नावली - ॥२०॥
"साधनसम्पन्नः सन्
गुरुशास्त्रादात्मानात्मविवेकं
कृत्वाऽत्मसाक्षात्कारो भवति।
"ब्रह्मेव सन् ब्रह्माप्येती"ति
श्रुतेः। तस्मादात्मज्ञानाद-
विद्याया निवृत्तिरेव मोक्षः।"

(क) शाङ्करभाष्य on ब्रह्मसूत्र १/१/१. पृ० ४९
cf. "ज्ञानेन हि प्रमाणेनावगन्तुमिष्टं ब्रह्म। ब्रह्मावगतिर्हि पुरुषार्थः। निःशेषसंसारवीजाद्यविद्याद्यनर्थहेतुनिवर्हणात्।"
(ख) शाङ्करभाष्य on ब्रह्मसूत्र १/१/४। पृ० १०५॥
cf. "ब्रह्मभावश्च मोक्षः।"

---

15. *On this point our present text has strong affinity with that of *Tattvānusandhānam*. It is to be noted here that both the text bears the same quotation from *Pañcadaśī*. On the discussion of this point, both the authors have been influenced by Vidyāraṇya Muni, the author of *Pañcadaśī*.

(ग) गौड़पादीयमाण्डूक्यकारिका - १/१६
(घ) प्रकटार्थविवरणम् - पृ० ४, ३४
(ङ) बृहदारण्यकभाष्यवार्त्तिकम् - २/४/१३८
(च) पंचदशी - ६/२१०, ७/२१२, १०/४
(छ) वेदान्तपरिभाषा - प्रयोजनपरिच्छेदः पृ० १६८
(ज) अद्वैतसिद्धिः पृ० ११६
(झ) आत्मबोधः ॥४४ ॥
(ञ) सिद्धान्तबिन्दु ॥१०७ ॥

18. ज्ञानम् —

*1. कियन्ति ज्ञानानि ?
प्रश्नावली - ॥२१ ॥ तत्त्वानुसन्धानम् - १म परिः पृ० १५

2. तेषां स्वरूपं किम् ?
प्रश्नावली - ॥२२ ॥

---

18. *On this point, the present text puts forth two questions; (1) how many types of knowledge are there? and (2) what individual form they possessed of ?

Jaḍa-Bharata recognizes two main sections of knowledge, the absolute and the empirical. The absolute is only one whereas the empirical knowledge are numorous in number.

According to Advaita-Vedānta the knowledge is only one and without a second, i.e., self-realization/salvation. In that case, Jaḍa-Bharata in his work tries to present something different from the traditional belief. But this difference is apparent. If the empirical existence of the world is taken for granted, then the concept of numerous empirical knowledge according to the modification of the mind, is nothing absurd. *Tattvānusandhānam* also holds the same view.

Regarding the question of the individual form of knowledge, other texts like *Tattvānusandhānam*, etc., are silent.

19. जीवः —

1. कः जीवः

प्रश्नावली - ॥२३॥

(क) प्रकटार्थविवरणम् पृ० ३-४
(ख) पंचपादिका पृ० ३९
(ग) पंचपादिकाविवरणम् - पृ० २६४
(घ) विवरणप्रमेयसंग्रहः - पृ० १०८
(ङ) पंचदशी - १/१५-१७, ४/९-१०
(च) अद्वैतसिद्धिः - पृ० २०२
(छ) सिद्धान्तबिन्दुः - पृ० ४४८

2. तस्यार्थः किम् ?

प्रश्नावली - ॥२४॥

तत्त्वानुसन्धानम् - १म परिः पृ० १२

20. ईश्वरः -

1. कः ईश्वर ?

प्रश्नावली - ॥२५॥
"मायोपाधिकचतैन्यमीश्वरः।" "मायां तु प्रकृतिं विद्यान्मायिनं तु महेश्वरमि"ति श्रुतेरयमीश्वरः।"

(क) तत्त्वानुसन्धानम् - १म परिः पृ० ३
cf. "एवंच मायोपहितचैतन्यमीश्वरो . . . मायां तु प्रकृतिं विद्यान्मायिनं तु महेश्वरमिति . . .।"
(ख) अद्वैतसिद्धिः - पृ० १९८
cf. "तत्रकारणोपाधिभूतमायोपहितं चैतन्यमीश्वरः।"
(ग) सर्ववेदान्तसिद्धान्तसारसंग्रहः - ३३६
cf. "अनन्तशक्तिसम्पन्नो मायोपाधिक ईश्वरः।"
(घ) पंचदशी - १/१६, ३/४०
(ङ) अनुभूतिप्रकाशः - १०/६१

2. तस्यार्थः किम् ?

प्रश्नावली - ॥२६॥
"पूर्वोक्तेश्वरस्यार्थो द्विविधः। वाच्यार्थो लक्ष्यार्थश्च। जगदुत्पत्तिस्थिति प्रलयस्थानं

(क) तत्त्वानुसन्धानम् - १म परिः पृ० १
cf. "स च द्विविधः। वाच्यार्थो लक्ष्यार्थश्चेति। मायोपहितं चैतन्यं तत्पदवाच्यार्थः, माया विनिर्मुक्तं चैतन्यं तत्पदलक्ष्यार्थः।"
(ख) पंचदशी - १/४४, ४८

सदन्तर्यामित्वसर्वज्ञत्व-सर्वेश्वरत्वादि गुणसंयुक्तं चैतन्यमविविक्तं सद्वाच्यार्थः। विविक्तं सदखण्ड चैतन्य लक्ष्यार्थो भवत्ययमीश्वरार्थः।"

cf. "जगतो यदुपादानं मायामादाय तामसीम्।निमित्तं शुद्धसत्त्वां तामुच्यते ब्रह्मतद्गिरा॥ मायाऽविद्ये विहायैवमुपाधी-परजीवयोः। अखण्डं सच्चिदानन्दं परं ब्रह्मैव लक्ष्यते॥"

21. संशयः -
*के संशयाः ?
प्रश्नावली - ॥२७॥ (क) तत्त्वानुसन्धानम् - ३य परिः - पृ० ३३

22. विपर्ययः -
किं विपर्ययः ?
प्रश्नावली - ॥२८॥ (क) तत्त्वानुसन्धानम् - ३य परिः - पृ० ३४

23. ब्रह्म —
1. किं ब्रह्म ?
प्रश्नावली - ॥२९॥
(क) शांकरभाष्य on ब्रह्मसूत्र १/१/१
(ख) भामती - पृ० २
(ग) पंचपादिका - पृ० ७०
(घ) पंचदशी - २/२० - २६
(ङ) अज्ञानबोधिनी - ॥५३॥
(च) वेदान्तसारः ॥१॥ पृ० १
(छ) सर्ववेदान्तसिद्धान्तसारसंग्रह ॥२॥ पृ० १

2. किं तस्य स्वरूपम् ?
प्रश्नावली - ॥३०॥
(क) तैत्तिरीयोपनिषत् २/१/१, २/५/१
(ख) छान्दोग्योपनिषत् ३/१४/१
(ग) बृहदारण्यकोपनिषत् २/५/१९
(घ) मुण्डकोपनिषत् ५/४
(ङ) आत्मनिरूपणम् ॥४४॥
(च) पंचपादिका ॥१॥ पृ० १
(छ) ब्रह्मसिद्धिः ॥१॥ पृ० १
(ज) भामती ॥१॥ पृ० १

---

21. **Praśnāvalī* presents here a modified version of *Tattvānusandhānam*.

24. उपसत्तिः -
*का उपसत्तिः ?
प्रश्नावली - ॥३१॥

25. एकपरत्व —
*किमेकपरत्वम् ?
प्रश्नावली - ॥३२॥

26. अनुभवः -
*कः अनुभवार्थः ?
प्रश्नावली - ॥३३॥

---

24 *On this point Jaḍa-Bharata presents a new technical term which is less-known in the classical or other Vedānta texts. In the Upaniṣads or other Vedānta texts like *Siddhāntaleśa*, etc. We find the use of the word *upasadaṇam* but not *upasatti* in the sense of going or approaching the teacher to learn any branch of science.

According to the derivation *upastti* should mean same as *upasadanam* but Jaḍa-Bharata used the term in a slight different way. By this term he meant not only to approach the teacher but also to receive the instruction from the teacher in the prescribed way. The aspirant, who is engrossed in *Brahman*, should receive this instruction.

25. *On this point, our concerned text presents a new term only. The thorough study of other Vedānta texts like *Pañcadaśī*, *Tattvānusandhānam*, etc., prove that the same topic is discussed but none of them used this particular term. *Bhāratītīrtha* calls it as *Brahmābhyāsa* (*Pañcadaśī*, 7/106, 13/83), whereas *Tattvānusandhānam* terms it as *abhyāsa* (*Tatt. Up.*, Chap. IV, p. 41) only. Jaḍa-Bharata contributed here a name only.

26. *On this point also Jaḍa-Bharata introduced a new name of a famous point of monistic philosophy. Because *anubhava* is nothing but the "Transcendental Realization," which being the central point of Advaita philosophy, have been discussed frequently in various books. But no other author explained the point according to this very name *anubhava*.

27. लक्षणा —
*का लक्षणा वृत्तिः ?
प्रश्नावली - ॥३४॥ (क) वेदान्तसारः - ॥११८-१२२॥
(ख) सर्ववेदान्तसिद्धान्तसारसंग्रहः।७३५-७३९।
(ग) स्वात्मनिरूपणम् - ३१-३७
(घ) तत्त्वानुसन्धानम् - २यः परिः, पृ० १९

28. प्रमाणम् —
कानि प्रमाणानि ?
प्रश्नावली ॥३८॥ तार्किकरक्षा - पृ० ५६

29. शिष्यः -
*कः शिष्यार्थः ?
प्रश्नावली -॥३९॥ (क) मुण्डकोपनिषत् - १/२/१३
(ख) वेदान्तसारः - ॥३०॥

30. गुरुः -
*1. कः गुरोरर्थः ?
प्रश्नावली -॥४०॥ वेदान्तसारः -॥३०॥
**2. किं तस्य लक्षणम् ?

---

27. *Here the question demands the definition of *lakṣaṇā* but Jaḍa-Bharata has shown its three divisions and the scope of *jahadajahallakṣaṇā*, in ascertaining the true import of *tattvamasi* and *aham brahmāsmi* thereby.

29. *To this point Jaḍa-Bharata doesn't show any originality but quotes a famous line from *Upadeśasāhasrī* (16/72) and thereby a qualified student of Vedānta is meant as a *śiṣya*.

30. *It is interesting to note here that although the question demands the meaning of the term *guru*, still our author goes on narrating the necessary qualities, required for being a *guru* and explains the derivative meaning of the term in the next question.

**In order to narrate the defining characteristics of *guru*, Jaḍa-Bharata has modified the view presented by *Vedāntasāra* and explained the term according to *Gurugītā*.

प्रश्नावली - ॥४१॥	(क) वेदान्तसारः ॥३०॥ (ख) श्री श्रीगुरुगीता ॥१७-१९॥

31. आत्मा —
क आत्मार्थः ?

प्रश्नावली - ॥४१॥	(क) ब्रह्मसूत्र - २/३/१७ (ख) शांकरभाष्य on ब्रह्मसूत्र २/३/१७ पृ० ५९३ (ग) शांकरभाष्य on ब्रह्मसूत्र १/१/१ पृ० ८०-८१ (घ) पंचपादिका - पृ० ७५ (ङ) आत्मज्ञानोपदेशविधिः - ४र्थ अः ॥१, १२॥ (च) सर्व्वेदान्तसिद्धान्तसारसंग्रहः - ॥४५८-४५९॥

32. परमात्मा —
कः परमात्मार्थः ?

प्रश्नावली - ॥४३॥	(क) श्रीमद्भगवद्गीता - १३/३२ (ख) उपदेश-साहस्री ॥१९॥ (ग) सर्ववेदान्तसिद्धान्तसारसंग्रहः ॥६७४॥ (घ) वाक्यवृत्तिः - ॥३०॥

33. सन्न्यासः -
*कः सन्न्यासार्थः ?

प्रश्नावली - ॥४४॥	(क) तत्त्वानुसन्धानम् - २य परिः पृ० २२ (ख) श्रीमद्भगवद्गीता - ५/१३, ६/१-२, १८/२ (ग) सन्न्यासोपनिषत् - २/१८, २३, पृ० २४८-५१ (घ) नारदपरिव्राजकोपनिषत् - ५/२-७ पृ० ९०-९४ (ङ) भिक्षुकोपनिषत् ।१। पृ० १९५

---

33. *On this point Jaḍa-Bharata didn't define the term according to the question, but has shown the four divisions, not that of *saṁnyāsa* but of the *saṁnyāsī* and at last defined the term according to *Gītā*.

34. त्यागः —
*कस्त्यागार्थः ?
प्रश्नावली - ॥४५॥ (क) श्रीमद्भगवद्गीता - १८/२-९
(ख) गूढ़ार्थदीपिका टीका on गीता on the above-cited verse: पृ० १०८१

35. स्वरूपः -
*कः स्वरूपार्थः ?
प्रश्नावली - ॥४६॥

36. अकर्ता —
*कः अकर्त्रर्थः ?
प्रश्नावली - ॥४७॥ (क) श्रीमद्भगवद्गीता - ३/२७, ४/१३-१४, १३/४०, १८/१७
(ख) पंचदशी - ७/८-९, १९३

37. वस्तु —
*कः वस्त्वर्थः ?
प्रश्नावली ॥४८॥ वेदान्तसारः - ॥३३॥

---

34. *Here our author presents a modified version of *Śrīmad-Bhagavad-Gītā* and *Gūḍhārthadīpikā ṭīkā* thereon.

35. *It is interesting to note here that by the term *svarūpa* actually our author wanted to mean the esence of self, in which the body, sense-organ, etc., on account of their being superimposed are regarded as *ātman*. Actually it is the indwelling self, the *pratyagātman*. The theory of *pratyagātman* is explained by former authors but none of them has termed it as such. Jaḍa-Bharata used the term, as a synonymn of the self. Herein lies his originality.

36. *Here *Praśnāvalī* explains the term with the help of *Gītā* (13/30, 18/17) and doesn't present any original view. It is another synonymn of *ātman*.

37. *It is *ātman*, the *sākṣin*, which is meant by the term *vastu*.

38. चित् —
कः चिदर्थः ?
प्रश्नावली - ॥४९॥

(क) कठोपनिषत् - २/२/१५
(ख) मुण्डकोपनिषत् २/२/१०
(ग) श्वेताश्वतरोपनिषत् - ६/१४
(घ) सर्ववेदान्तसिद्धान्तसारसंग्रहः ॥६१०, ६१२, ६१९-६२७॥
(ङ) पंचदशी - ॥३/१६, १०/९-११॥
(च) स्वात्मप्रकाशिका - ॥९॥, ॥१७॥
(छ) आत्मानात्मविवेकः - पृ० ३९

39. आनन्दः -
*कः आनन्दार्थः ?
प्रश्नावली - ॥४९॥

(क) मुण्डकोपनिषत् - ५/४
(ख) तैत्तिरीयोपनिषत् - २/४, ३/६।
(ग) बृहदारण्यकोपनिषत् - ४/५/६।
(घ) ब्रह्मसूत्र - १/१/१२
(ङ) पंचदशी - ११/५, ११, १३; १२/६९, १३/३
(च) वेदान्तसिद्धान्तमुक्तावली ॥४४-४५॥
(छ) सर्ववेदान्तसिद्धान्तसारसंग्रहः ॥६१४-६३२॥

40. अनन्तः -
को अनन्तार्थः ?
प्रश्नावली - ॥५१॥

(क) तत्वानुसन्धानम् - १म परिः पृ० १३
(ख) सर्ववेदान्तसिद्धान्तसारसंग्रह- ६७८-६७९
(ग) पंचदशी - २/१५-२१, ३/३६

---

*39. On this point the concerned text doesn't contribute anything original but uses lots of quotations from *Pañcadaśī*, *Bṛhadāraṇyakopaniṣat*, *Taittirīyopaniṣat*, etc., and thereby explains the term.

Glossary

अकर्ता (*akartā*)	:	Non-agent.
अकर्त्रर्थ (*akartrartha*)	:	True import of the term *akartṛ*.
अक्षर (*akṣara*)	:	Imperishable, immutable.
अखण्ड (*akhaṇḍa*)	:	Indivisible, undivided.
अखण्ड चैतन्य (*akhaṇḍa-caitanya*)	:	Indivisible Consciousness.
अचित् (*acit*)	:	Insentient, inert, non-consciousness.
अच्युत (*acyuta*)	:	Infallible.
अजहल्लक्षणा (*ajahallakṣaṇā*)	:	Non-exclusive implication.
अज्ञान (*ajñāna*)	:	Nescience.
अण्डज (*aṇḍaja*)	:	Egg-born body.
अद्वय (*advaya*)	:	One, unique.
अधिकारी (*adhikārī*)	:	Eligible person.
अध्यास (*adhyāsa*)	:	Superimposition.
अनन्त (*ananta*)	:	Infinite.
अनन्तार्थ (*anantārtha*)	:	Meaning of the term *ananta*.
अनर्थ (*anartha*)	:	Evil, suffering.
अनात्म (*anātma*)	:	Non-self.
अनात्मबुद्धि (*anātmabuddhi*)	:	To take as non-self.
अनात्मस्मृति (*anātma-smṛti*)	:	Memory about non-self.
अनादि (*anādi*)	:	Beginningless.

अनित्य (*anitya*)	:	Impermanent, transitory.
अनुबन्ध चतुष्टय (*anubandha catuṣṭaya*)	:	Four prerequisites necessary for philosophical work, viz., (1) subject (*viṣaya*), (2) necessity (*prayojana*), (3) relation (*sambandha*), and (4) eligible student (*adhikārī*).
अनुभव (*anubhava*)	:	Knowledge, realization, experience.
अनेकजीववाद (*anekajīvavāda*)	:	The theory of multiple soul.
अन्तर्यामिन् (*antaryāmin*)	:	The indweller, the inner-guide, the cosmic form of the self associated with *māyā*.
अन्नमय कोष (*annamaya koṣa*)	:	The sheath of food. It is the outermost sheath enveloping the individual soul.
अपवाद (*apavāda*)	:	De-superimposition.
अपंचीकृत (*apañcīkṛta*)	:	Non-quintuplicated.
अभिभूत (*abhibhūta*)	:	Being overcome.
अयथार्थ (*ayathārtha*)	:	Erroneous.
अयथार्थस्मृति (*ayathārtha-smṛti*)	:	Erroneous memory.
अवच्छेदवाद (*avacchedavāda*)	:	The theory of limitation.
अविद्या (*avidyā*)	:	Ignorance, nescience.
अविविक्त (*avivikta*)	:	Non-differentiated.
अविवेक (*aviveka*)	:	Non-discrimination.
अहंकार (*ahaṅkāra*)	:	Egoism, the concept of individuality.
आगामीकर्म (*āgāmī-karma*)	:	Future deed.
आत्मगत (*ātmagata*)	:	About self.

आत्मतत्त्व (*ātmatattva*) : Theory of self.

आत्मसाक्षात्कार (*ātma-sākṣātkāra*) : Self-realization.

आत्मस्मृति (*ātma-smṛti*) : Memory about self.

आत्मा (*ātmā*) : Self, soul.

आत्मार्थ (*ātmārtha*) : True import of the term *ātman*.

आत्मानात्मविवेक (*ātmānātmaviveka*) : Differentiation between self and non-self.

आध्यासिक (*ādhyāsika*) : Superimposed.

आनन्द (*ānanda*) : Bliss, delight.

आनन्दार्थ (*ānandārtha*) : Connotation of the term *ānanda*.

आनन्दमय कोष (*ānandamaya koṣa*) : The sheath of bliss. The innermost of the five sheaths enveloping the self.

आभासवाद (*ābhāsavāda*) : Theory of appearance.

आरम्भवाद (*ārambhavāda*) : Theory of origination.

आवरण-शक्ति (*āvaraṇa-śakti*) : Power of concealment or enveloping.

इह (*iha*) : Worldly.

इहामुत्रार्थ-फलभोगविराग (*ihāmutrārtha-phalabhogavirāga*) : Renunciation of the enjoyment of the results of actions in this world and the world hereafter.

ईश/ईश्वर (*īśa/īśvara*) : God, Highest Soul.

ईश्वरगत (*īśvaragata*) : Relating to god.

ईश्वरोपाधि (*īśvaropādhi*) : Adjunct of god.

उपरति (*uparati*) : Desisting from the sensual enjoyment or any worldly action.

उपसत्ति (*upasatti*) : The act of approaching respectfully.

उपसन्न (***upasanna***)	:	One, who has come near.
उपहित (***upahita***)	:	Ascribed, imposed.
उपादान (***upādāna***)	:	Casual substance, material cause.
उपाधि (***upādhi***)	:	Limiting adjunct.
उपासना (***upāsanā***)	:	Contemplation or meditation on *Brahman* by the aid of symbols advised by *śruti*.
एकतार्थ (***ekatārtha***)	:	Meaning of the term *ekatā*.
एकपरत्व (***ekaparatva***)	:	To be engrossed in one.
एकजीववाद (***ekajīvavāda***)	:	The theory of single soul.
ऐक्य (***aikya***)	:	Oneness, unity.
ऐक्यगत (***aikyagata***)	:	About unification.
कर्ता (***kartā***)	:	Agent.
कर्म (***karma***)	:	Action, rites.
कर्माध्यक्ष (***karmādhyakṣa***)	:	The ordainer of deeds.
कर्मेन्द्रिय पंचक (***karmendriya pañcaka***)	:	Five organs of action.
कारण (***kāraṇa***)	:	Cause.
कारणोपाधि (***kāraṇopādhi***)	:	Adjunct of the cause.
कारणोपहित (***kāraṇopahita***)	:	Associated with cause.
कार्य (***kārya***)	:	Effect.
कार्योपाधि (***kāryopādhi***)	:	Adjunct of the effect.
कार्योपहित (***kāryopahita***)	:	Ascribed to the effect.
कुटीचक (***kuṭīcaka***)	:	A type of religious mendicant, who lives at his son's expense.
कुतर्क (***kutarka***)	:	Illogical reasoning.
कूटस्थचैतन्य (***kūṭastha-caitanya***)	:	Immutable Consciousness.

केवलज्ञान (*kevala-jñāna*) :	Direct knowledge, immediate perception.
कोष (*koṣa*) :	Sheath.
गुरु (*guru*) :	Preceptor.
गूढाशय (*gūḍhāśaya*) :	Concealing one's intention.
चित्, चित्शक्ति (*cit, cit-śakti*):	Consciousness, power of consciousness.
चिदचित् (*cidacit*) :	Sentient and insentient.
चिदर्थ (*cidartha*) :	Connotation of the term *cit*.
चिदाभास (*cidābhāsa*) :	The reflection of intelligence which resides in the internal organ.
चिद्रूप (*cidrūpa*) :	Consciousness itself.
जगत् प्रपंच (*jagat prapañca*):	Worldly appearance.
जन्य (*janya*) :	Producible things.
जरायुज (*jarāyuja*) :	Womb-born beings.
जहत्लक्षणा (*jahatlakṣaṇā*):	Exclusive implication which gives away its literal meaning.
ज्ञान (*jñāna*) :	knowledge.
ज्ञाननिवर्त्त्य (*jñānanivarttya*):	Removable by knowledge.
ज्ञानाधिकरण (*jñānādhikaraṇa*):	Locus of knowledge.
ज्ञानावरणीय (*jñānāvaraṇīya*):	Knowledge obscuring.
ज्ञानेन्द्रिय (*jñānendriya*) :	Sense-organ.
ज्ञानोपहित (*jñānopahita*) :	Superimposed to the soul.
जाति (*jāti*) :	Universal.
जीव, जीव-चैतन्य (*jīva, jīva-caitanya*) :	Individual self.
जीवन्मुक्त (*jīvan-mukta*) :	Liberated or emancipated while alive.

तटस्थ लक्षण (*taṭastha lakṣaṇa*): Accidental attributes.

तन्मात्र (*tanmātra*) : The subtle essence of elements.

तमः (*tamaḥ*) : The quality of darkness, inertia.

तादात्म्य (*tādātmya*) : Identity.

तामस (*tāmasa*) : Delusive.

तारतम्य (*tāratamya*) : Difference.

तितिक्षा (*titikṣā*) : Forbearance, endurance of opposites.

तुलाऽज्ञानम् (*tulā'jñānam*) : Subsidiary nescience.

त्यागार्थ (*tyāgārtha*) : Renunciation.

त्रिकोषात्मक (*trikoṣātmaka*): Having three sheaths.

त्रिवृत्करण (*trivṛtkaraṇa*) : Triplication.

दम (*dama*) : Self-control.

दुराग्रह (*durāgraha*) : Mis-apprehension.

दृक् (*dṛk*) : Perceiving consciousness.

दृश्य (*dṛśya*) : Objects of consciousness.

द्रष्टा (*draṣṭā*) : Pure consciousness comprehending all objects.

नित्य (*nitya*) : Eternal.

नित्यानित्यवस्तुविवेक (*nityānityavastuviveka*) : Discrimination between eternal and transitory objects.

निदिध्यासन (*nididhyāsana*): Meditation.

निवृत्ति (*nivṛtti*) : Cessation.

निमित्त कारण (*nimitta kāraṇa*): Instrumental cause.

निर्गुण ब्रह्म (*nirguṇa brahman*) : Attributeless *Brahman*.

निरुपाधिक भ्रम : Error without adjunct.

(***nirupādhika bhrama***)		
निष्प्रपंच (***niṣprapañca***)	:	Trans-phenomenol.
निषिद्धकर्म (***niṣiddha-karma***)	:	Prohibited rites.
नैमित्तिक-कर्म (***naimittika-karma***)	:	Occasional rites.
न्यास (***nyāsa***)	:	Resigning, puttting away
पंचकोष (***pañcakoṣa***)	:	Five sheathes.
पंचकोषात्मक (***pañcakoṣātmaka***)	:	Having five sheaths.
पंच तन्मात्र (***pañca tanmātra***)	:	Five rudimentary elements.
पंचभूत (***pañcabhūta***)	:	Five elements.
पंचीकरण (***pañcīkaraṇa***)	:	Quintuplication.
पंचीकृत (***pañcīkṛta***)	:	Quintuplicated.
परमात्मा (***paramātmā***)	:	Supreme Soul.
परमात्मार्थ (***paramātmārtha***)	:	Connotation of the term *paramātman*.
परिणाम (***pariṇāma***)	:	Modification, evolution.
परिणामवाद् (***pariṇāmavāda***)	:	Theory of evolution.
पारमार्थिक (***pāramārthika***)	:	Absolute.
प्रकृति (***parkṛti***)	:	Primordial substance.
प्रज्ञा (***prajñā***)	:	Intellect.
प्रज्ञामान्द्य (***prajñāmāndya***)	:	Dullness of intellect.
प्रतिबन्ध (***pratibandha***)	:	Obstacle, impediment.
प्रतिबिम्ब (***pratibimba***)	:	Reflection.
प्रतिबिम्बवाद् (***pratibimbavāda***)	:	Theory of reflection.
प्रत्यगात्मा (***pratyagātmā***)	:	Indwelling self.
प्रत्यभिज्ञा (***pratyabhijñā***)	:	Recognition.

प्रधान (***pradhāna***)	:	Primordial substance.
प्रपंच (***prapañca***)	:	Wordly appearance.
प्रमाण (***pramāṇa***)	:	Source of knowledge.
प्रमाता (***pramātā***)	:	Knower.
प्रयोजन (***prayojana***)	:	Necessity.
प्रलय (***pralaya***)	:	Dissolution.
प्राणमय कोष (***prāṇamaya koṣa***)	:	Vital sheath.
प्रारब्ध (***prārabdha***)	:	Past deed.
बन्ध (***bandha***)	:	Bondage.
बुद्धि (***buddhi***)	:	Intellect.
बुद्धिमन्दता (***buddhimandatā***)	:	Dullness of intellect.
ब्रह्म (***brahma***)	:	*Brahman*, Highest Soul.
भावी प्रतिबन्ध (***bhāvī pratibandha***)	:	Future impediment.
भूत प्रतिबन्ध (***bhūta pratibandha***)	:	Arrear impediment.
भ्रम (***bhrama***)	:	Illusion, delusion.
मन (***mana***)	:	Mind, intellect.
मनन (***manana***)	:	Reasoning.
मनोमय कोष (***manomaya koṣa***)	:	Mental sheath.
महत् (***mahat***)	:	Cosmic intelligence, the first product of nature.
मानस (***mānasa***)	:	Mental, internal.
माया (***māyā***)	:	*māyā*.
मिथ्या (***mithyā***)	:	Illusory, false.

मुक्ति (***mukti***)	:	Liberation, emancipation.
मुमुक्षु (***mumukṣū***)	:	Aspirant after liberation.
मूलाऽज्ञानम् (***mūlā'jñānam***)	:	Primal nescience.
मेघाकाश (***meghākāśā***)	:	Sky associated with cloud.
मोक्ष (***mokṣa***)	:	Liberation.
रजः (***rajaḥ***)	:	Quality of activity.
रजस्तमोऽभिभूत (***rajastamo'bhibūta***)	:	Bewildered by *rajas* and *tamas*.
राजस (***rājasa***)	:	Pertaining to *rajas*.
लक्षणा (***lakṣaṇā***)	:	Implication.
लक्ष्यार्थ (***lakṣyārtha***)	:	Implied sense.
लय (***laya***)	:	Dissolution.
वर्ण (***varṇa***)	:	Race.
वाच्य (***vācya***)	:	Literal.
वाच्यार्थ (***vācyārtha***)	:	Literal sense.
विकार (***vikāra***)	:	Modification, alternation from the natural form, apparent transformation.
विक्षेप-शक्ति (***vikṣepa-śakti***)	:	Power of projection.
विज्ञानमय कोष (***vijñānamaya-koṣa***)	:	Intellectual sheath.
विपर्यय (***viparyaya***)	:	Misapprehension.
विवर्त (***vivarta***)	:	Apparent illusory form.
विवर्तवाद (***vivartavāda***)	:	Theory of illusory appearance superimposed by *māyā*.
विवेकिन् (***vivekin***)	:	The person having the power of discrimination.
विषयासक्ति (***viṣayāsakti***)	:	Attachment to the objects of sensual pleasure.

वृत्ति (*vṛtti*)	:	Modification.
वैराग्य (*vairāgya*)	:	Renunciation, Non-attachment.
बोध्यबोधकभाव (*bodhyabodhakabhāva*)	:	Relation between the things to be known and that which makes it known.
व्यावहारिक (*vyāvahārika*)	:	Empirical.
व्यष्टि (*vyaṣṭi*)	:	Individual.
व्यष्टिरूप अज्ञान (*vyaṣṭirūpa ajñāna*)	:	Individual nescience.
शम (*śama*)	:	Mental restraint.
शान्त (*śānta*)	:	The person having *śama*.
शुद्धसत्त्वप्रधान (*śuddhasattvapradhāna*)	:	Preponderance of pure *sattva*.
शुद्धान्तःकरण (*śuddhāntaḥkarṇa*)	:	Purified intellect.
श्रद्धा (*śraddhā*)	:	Faith.
श्रवण (*śravaṇa*)	:	Listening.
सगुण ब्रह्म (*saguṇa brahma*)	:	Determinate *Brahman*.
संवादि भ्रम (*saṁvādi bhrama*)	:	A kind of error which corresponds to the fact by way of chance/accident.
संशय (*saṁśaya*)	:	Doubt.
संस्कार (*saṁskāra*)	:	Impression.
सच्चिदानन्द (*saccidānanda*)	:	Being-consciousness-bliss.
सजातीयादिभेद (*sajātīyādibheda*)	:	Difference from the things of same genus, etc.
संचितकर्म (*sañcita-karma*)	:	Accumulated deed.
सत्त्व (*sattva*)	:	The first of the three qualities of

		prakr̥ti, which stands for purity and intelligence.
संन्यास (***saṁnyāsa***)	:	Renunciation.
समष्टिरूप अज्ञान (***samaṣṭirūpa ajñāna***)	:	Collective ignorance.
समाधान (***samādhāna***)	:	Self-settledness.
सम्बन्ध (***sambandha***)	:	Relation.
सम्भव (***sambhava***)	:	Inclusion, equivalence, one of the eight *pramāṇa*s.
सर्वज्ञत्व (***sarvajñatva***)	:	Omniscience.
सर्वभूताधिवासः (***sarvabhūtādhivāsaḥ***)	:	One, who dwells in all beings.
सर्वभूतान्तरात्मा (***sarvabhūtāntarātmā***)	:	Inner self of everybody.
सर्वेश्वरत्व (***sarveśvaratva***)	:	Universal.
साक्षी (***sākṣī***)	:	Witness.
सात्त्विक (***sāttvika***)	:	Illuminating.
साधनचतुष्टय (***sādhanacatuṣṭaya***)	:	Four *sādhana*s.
सूक्ष्म-शरीर (***sūkṣma-śarīra***)	:	Subtle-body.
सोपाधिक भ्रम (***sopādhika bhrama***)	:	Error having adjunct.
स्थूल-शरीर (***sthūla-śarīra***)	:	Gross-body.

Bibliography

Anubhūti Svarūpācārya, *Prakaṭārthavivaraṇam,* ed. T.R. Chintamani, Madras University Sanskrit Series No. 9, vol. 1, Madras: University of Madras, 1935.

Appaya Dīkṣita, *Siddhāntaleśasaṁgraha,* ed. with Kṛṣṇālaṅkāraṭīkā of Acyuta Kṛṣṇālaṅkāra by P.P.S. Shastri, Sri Vani Vilas Sastra Series, Srirangam: Sri Vani Vilas Press, 1935.

Apte, V.S., *Students' Sanskrit-English Dictionary,* Delhi: Motilal Banarsidass, 1890, 2nd edn, 1982.

Aśvaghoṣa, *Vajrasūcī,* ed. with trans. S.K. Mukhopadhyaya, Sino-Indian Studies No. 2, Shantiniketan: Sino-Indian Cultural Society, 1950, 2nd rev. edn., 1960.

Aufrecht, Theodor, *Catalogus Catalogorum,* Delhi: Indological Book House, 1891, rpt. 1989.

Bādarāyaṇa, *Brahmasūtra,* ed. with the commentaries of Śaṅkara, Bhāmatī Kalpataru and Parimala by K.L. Joshi, Parimal Sanskrit Series No. 1, vol. I, II, Delhi: Parimal Publications, 1981, 2nd edn., rpt. 1982.

Bhagavadgītā, trans. with the commentary of Śaṅkarācārya Swāmī Gambhīrānanda, Mayavati, Pithoragarh: Advaita Ashrama, 1984.

Bṛhadāraṇyakopaniṣat, ed. with the Commentary of Śaṅkara and a gloss of Ānandagiri by Kāśīnātha Śāstrī Āgashe, Anandashrama Sanskrit Granthavali No. 15, Poona: Anandasrama Press, 1914.

Chāndogyopaniṣat, ed. with the Commentary of Śaṅkara and a gloss of Ānandagiri, by E. Röer, Bibliotheeca Indica Series No. 3, Calcutta: Asiatic Society, 1850.

Citsukhācārya, *Tattvapradīpikā,* ed. Kaśīnātha Śāstrī, Bombay: Nirnaya Sagar Press, 1915.

Dharmarājādhvarīndra, *Vedāntaparibhāṣā,* ed. and tr. S.S. Surya Nārāyaṇa Śāstrī, The Adyar Library Series No. 34, Madras: The Adyar Library and Research Centre, 1942, rpt. 1984.

Dharmarājādhvarīndra, *Vedāntaparibhāṣa,* ed. with Arthabodhinī-ṭīkā by Sri Srimohan Tarkavedantatirtha Bhattacharya, Calcutta, 1970.

Grimns, John, *A Concise Dictionary of Indian Philosophy* (*Sans.-Eng.*) Madras University Series No. 48, Madras: Radhakrishnan Institute for Advanced Study in Philosophy, University of Madras, 1988.

Hultzsch, E., "Notice on Indian Manuscripts," *Zeitschrift der Deutschen Morgenländischen Gesselschaft*, vol. 40, part 1, Leipzig, 1886.

Jacob, Colonel G.A., *A Concordance to the Principal Upaniṣads and Bhagavadgītā*, Delhi: Motilal Banarsidass, 1891, rpt. 1985.

Katre, S.M., *Introduction to Indian Textual Criticism*, Deccan College Handbook Series, 5, Poona: Deccan College Post Graduate and Research Institute, 1954, 2nd edn., rpt. 1981.

Mahābharata, ed. V.S. Sukthankar *et al.*, vol. 13-17, Śāntiparvan, Anuśāsanaparvan, Pune: BORI, 1930-66.

Majjhima Nikāya, ed. Mp. Rāhula Sāṅkṛtyāyana Nalanda-Devnagari-Pali Series, vol. II, Majjhima Paṇṇāsakam, Bihar: Pali Publication Board, 1958.

Malalasekara, G.P., *Dictionary of Pali Proper Names*, Indian Text Series, Delhi: Oriental Reprint, 1937, rpt. 1983.

Māṇḍūkyopaniṣat, ed. with the commentary of Śaṅkara and a gloss of Ānandagiri by Durga Carana Sankhya-Vedantatirtha, Calcutta: 2nd edn. 1924.

Monier-Williams, Sir, *A Sanskrit-English Dictionary*, 1899, Delhi: Motilal Banarsidass, 1899, 9th rpt. 1984.

Mukhopadhyaya, Bijaya Nath, *Administration of Manuscript Libraries with Special Reference to Sanskrit Manuscripts*, Calcutta Sanskrit College Research Series No. CXXVIII, Calcutta: Sanskrit College, 1985.

Muṇḍakopaniṣat, ed. with the commentary of Śaṅkara and a gloss of Āanandagiri by Paṇḍits at Anandashrama, Anandashrama Sanskrit Granthavali No. 9, Poona: Anandashrama Press, 1915.

Nṛsiṁhapūrvottaratāpanīyopaniṣat, ed. Paṇḍits at Anandashrama, Anandashrama Sanskrit Granthavali No. 30, Pune: Anandashrama Press, 1985.

Padmapādācārya, *Pañcapādikā*, ed. Rama Shastri Bhagavatacharya, The Vizianagram Sanskrit Series No. 3, vol. II, Part 1, Banaras: E.J. Lazarus and Co., 1891.

Potter, Karl. H., *Encyclopaedia of Indian Philosophy*, vol. I, Bibliography, 1970, 2nd rev. edn., 1983, vol. III, Advaita-Vedanta, Delhi: Motilal Banarsidass, 1981.

Prakāśātman, *Pañcapādikāvivaraṇam*, ed. Rama Shastri Bhagvatacharya, The Vizianagram Sanskrit Series No. 5, vol III, Banaras: E.J. Lazarus and Co., 1892.

Radhakrishnan, S., *Principal Upaniṣads*, Delhi: Oxford University Press, 1953, rpt. 1989.

Raghavan, V., *New Catalogus Catalogorum*, vol. I, 1949 rpt. 1968; vol. VII, Madras: University of Madras, 1973.

Ṛgveda-Saṁhitā, ed. with the commentary of Sāyaṇācārya, by N.S. Sontakke, vols. 1-4, Pune: Vaidika Saṁśodhana Maṇḍala, 1935-1941 2nd ed. rpt. 1972-1984.

Sāmānyavedāntopaniṣad, ed. A. Mahadeva Shastri, Madras, Adyar Library, 1921.

Śaṅkarācārya, *Śaṅkara Granthamāla*, ed. Panchanana Tarkaratna, vol. II, III, Calcutta: Vasumati Sahitya Mandir, 1892, 8th edn., 1932.

Śaṅkarācārya, *Sarvavedāntasiddhāntasārasaṁgraha*, ed. and tr. Pramathanath Tarkabhushan, Calcutta: 2nd edn. 1964.

Śaṅkarācārya, *Upadeśasāhasrī*, ed. S. Subrahmanya Shastri, Advaita Grantha-Ratha-Mañjuṣā No. 15, Varanasi: Mahesh Research Institute, 1978.

Sankarananda and Mahadevendra Sarasvati *Brahmasūtradīpikā and Tattvānusandhānam*, ed. Ramashastri Tailanga, Banaras Sanskrit Series Nos. 91 and 112. Banares: Braj. B. Das and Co., 1906.

Sarasvati, Madhusudana, *Advaitasiddhi*, ed. P.N.S. Anantakrishna Shastri, Parimal Sanskrit Series No. 7, Delhi: Parimal Publications, 1982.

Sarasvati, (Swami) Prajnananda, *Vedāntadarśaner Itihāsa*, ed. Rajendra Nath Ghosh, Sankaramath Granthavali, 3 vols. Barisala: Sankaramath, 1925.

Sarasvati, Sadananda Yogindra, *Vedāntasāra*, ed. with Subodhinī-ṭīkā of Nṛsiṁha Sarasvatī, Bālabodhinī-ṭīkā of Śrī Āpodeva and Vidvānmanorañjinī-ṭīkā of Rāmatīrtha Yati by Brahmachari Medhacaitanya, Calcutta, 1968.

Sarasvati, Sadananda Yogindra, *Vedāntasāra*, ed. and trans. Swami Nikhilananda, Mayabati, Pithoragarh: Advaita Asrama, 1949, 8th edn., rpt. 1987.

Sarvajñātman, *Saṁkṣepaśārīrakam*, ed. with Sārasaṁgraha ṭīkā of Madhusudana Sarasvati by Bhan Shastri Vajhe, Kashi Sanskrit Series (Haridas Sanskrit Granthamala) No. 18, Vedanta Section No. 4 Benares: Chowkhamba Sanskrit Series Office, 1924.

Shastri, Kokileshwar, *A Realistic Interpretation to Sankara Vedanta*, Sri Gopal Basu Mallick Fellowship Lectures, Calcutta: University of Calcutta, 1931-32.

Shastri, Ashutosh, *Vedāntadarśana: Advaitavāda*, Bharatiya Dersana-Granthamala, vol. I, Calcutta, University of Calcutta, 1942.

Shastri, (MMP) Haraprasad, *A Descriptive Catalogue of Sanskrit Manuscripts of the Asiatic Society*, vol. XI, Calcutta: The Asiatic Society, 1957.

Śrī Śrī Gurugītā, ed. Ashvini Kumar Bhattacharya, Calcutta, 1915.

Śrīmad Bhagavadgītā, ed. with a gloss of Madhusudana Sarasvati by Nalinikanta Brahma, trans. Bhutanath Saptatirtha, Calcutta, Naba-Bharata Publishers, 1986.

Śvetāśvataropaniṣat, ed. with the commentary of Śaṅkara by Pandits at Anandashrama, Anandashrama Sanskrit Granthavali No. 17, Poona: Anandashrama Press, 1905.

Sureśvarācārya, *Naiṣkarmyasiddhi*, ed. Colonel G.A. Jacob, Bombay Sanskrit and Prakrit Series No. XXXVIII, Poona: Bhandarkar Oriental Research Institute, 1890, 4th edn. 1980.

Taittirīyopaniṣat, ed. with the commentary of Śaṅkara and a gloss of Ānandagiri by Pandits at Anandashrama, Anandashrama Sanskrit Granthavali No. 12, Pune: Anandashrama Press, 1922.

Upaniṣad Granthāvalī, ed. Swami Jagadananda, tr. Swami Gambhirananda. 3 vols., Calcutta, Udbodhana Karyalaya, 1941, 11th edn., rpt. 1987.

Upaṇiṣadāṁ Samuccayaḥ, ed. with commentary and Dipika of Nārāyaṇa Paṇḍita and Śaṅkarānanda, by Pandits at Anandashrama, Anandashrama Sanskrit Granthavali No. 29, Pune: Anandashrama Press, No. date.

Unaviṁśati-Saṁhitā, ed. and tr. Panchanana Tarkaratna, Calcutta, 1907.

Vedāntadarśanam, ed. with Śārīrakabhāṣya of Śaṅkara and Bhāmatī of Vachaspati Mishra by Durga Carana Sankhya Vedantatirtha, trans. Kalivara Vedantavagisa, 4 vols., Cacutta: 1969.

Vidyāraṇyamuni, *Pañcadaśī*, ed. with tr. Swami Swahananda, Madras: Sri Rama-Krishna Math, 1967, 4th ed. rpt. 1987.

Vidyāraṇyamuni, *Vivaraṇaprameyasaṁgraha*, ed. with trans. Pramathanatha Tarkabhushana, Calcutta: Vasumati Sahitya Mandir, 1927.

Vimuktātman, *Iṣṭasiddhi*, ed. M.K. Hiriyanna, Gaekwad's Oriental Series No. LXV, Baroda: Oriental Institute, 1933.